DON'T
FEED THE
ELEPHANTS!

DON'T
FEED THE
ELEPHANTS!

Overcoming the Art of Avoidance
to Build Powerful Partnerships

SARAH NOLL WILSON

LIONCREST
PUBLISHING

DON'T FEED THE ELEPHANTS!
Overcoming the Art of Avoidance to Build Powerful Partnerships

ISBN   978-1-5445-2512-9   *Hardcover*

978-1-5445-2450-4   *Paperback*

978-1-5445-2449-8   *Ebook*

978-1-5445-2451-1   *Audiobook*

Contents

To Mom, Dad, and Nick. You support me relentlessly, wipe my tears compassionately, and listen to me talk (a lot). I wouldn't be who I am without you.

Foreword

By Dr. Cris Wildermuth

The first time I met Sarah, I was a brand-new Assistant Professor at Drake University, still finding my way around campus. I was scared, trying to figure out how far I could go before my academic colleagues would think I was too crazy. Imposter syndrome was rearing its ugly head. Am I truly qualified to be a professor? Do I deserve to be here? Will students be confused or bored? I was desperate for allies then, students who got my quirkiness and love for the unusual, humans unafraid of failure. Sarah was one of my first allies, and she has continued to be to this day.

Over the years, we've learned to share leadership, leading and following in a graceful dance. We love the story of the geese that fly in a V-formation, each goose flapping its wings and easing the others' burden. When the lead goose gets tired, two other geese stay behind to support the leader, and another goose takes over. We got used to just saying "Goose" to each other. We knew what that meant. One of us was tired; the other would keep going. To the teams we led, it felt seamless. Working with Sarah taught me that leadership is a journey to be shared, not a solitary endeavor.

About *Don't Feed the Elephants*

Let's face it: Most of us live in a world filled with judgment. We learn how to judge ourselves and others almost before we learn how to talk. Right. Wrong. Rule following. We discover how to fit in, avoid bothering the popular kids, and get decent grades. We protect ourselves by staying silent, ignoring persistent pain, and finding the one BFF with whom we can be vulnerable. By the time we are adults, we have become gourmet chefs, cooking exquisite peanut-based dishes for our elephant collection.

Like many of you, I am also an expert elephant feeder with a lifetime of experience raising peanut crops. I grew up in Brazil, and in my family, "thou shalt not be rude" was the eleventh commandment. My motto used to be "if you want to say something about me, go ahead and say it behind my back." So yes: I know every elephant feeding technique one could imagine. Feigning ignorance. Seething in silence. Telling friends about problems I'll never solve. But I don't know how to stop cooking new peanut dishes. I have, so far, failed at putting my elephants on a diet.

Sarah writes that we all have a choice: We can release our elephant or keep feeding it. Elephant feeding, however, is costly. Your peanut farms steal your energy, stifle creativity, and destroy trust and teamwork. We must get out of the peanut farming and gourmet peanut cooking business. Doing so will release the useless energy we spend on meetings behind meetings, venting without solutions, and gossiping without purpose.

There is more to this book, though, than enhancing teamwork. Unapologetically human, Sarah is unafraid of vulnerability. She shares raw experiences most of us would try to hide—moments of shame and fear, panic attacks, and self-doubt. Sarah's honesty gives her readers permission to capitalize on their own raw humanity. *Don't Feed the Elephants* will help you conquer your fears and speak your truth. In the end, you may find that this book will not only free the elephants but also release your own power.

Introduction

Of course, you know what an elephant is. Big, gray beast, long trunk, and large ears. They like peanuts, have a reputation for not forgetting anything and being afraid of mice.

To be clear, no one wants those real-life pachyderms to go unfed.

There's another kind of elephant that you're probably aware of too. It looks like avoidance of addressing a known conflict that creates a harmful barrier to success. It's big. It's there. It might be hanging out in the conference room under someone's chair, or even sprawled across the table. Everyone is aware of this elephant in the room, and no one's talking about it.

In fact, no one on your team is talking much at all. At least not about anything that matters. Your team is discouraged, disconnected, and disenchanted. No one challenges ideas to get to better solutions or discusses the difficulties they encounter on a project. They all say everything is fine...until it isn't, and you're stuck trying to solve problems that could have been avoided with better communication. Your most productive team lead gave notice last week. You're finding it hard to drag yourself into work in the morning. Something is getting in the way of your team's success, and it feels like everyone is spinning and getting nowhere. You'd fix it if you could, but you have no idea how to begin. I get it. I've been there too. Now, I coach executives and teams through these issues, and I'm here to help you too.

A REFORMED AVOIDER

For as long as I can remember, I've been passionate about solving problems and disrupting the status quo. I was especially fearless when it came to rules or expectations from authority that felt limiting. I was only ten years old when I was told that girls couldn't serve in the church as altar boys. I kept asking, "Why not?" and volunteering, never getting a chance or a reasonable explanation, until one fateful day when a fellow altar boy didn't show up. I was there with my robes on, ready to step in with a smile. Still one of my (and my parents') proudest moments growing up.

While I had many moments of speaking up and pushing against the boundaries of authority, that same courage didn't extend to my personal relationships. It's much easier to have courage when you have nothing to lose, but when it came to my most precious connections, I was a masterful avoider and smoother-over.*

*Smoother-over, by the way, is a very technical term for some-one who works hard to remove the discomfort in a situation by any means possible while not solving the issue at hand.

The impact of my avoidance was put on full display when I started dating Nick, the man who eventually became my husband. Before my relationship with Nick began, my avoidant tactics served to protect me and didn't impact others (or so I thought), but after meeting Nick, I learned that you can't hide in relationships. If you try to hide, you won't just avoid the conflict; you'll avoid trust and connection as well.

Nick and I had a consistent point of disagreement around how we spent time in our social lives. I resisted talking about it by employing my masterful avoidance skills. I would use classic moves like changing the subject ("What did the Royals do today?"), closing the door, ("I'm too tired to talk right now"), or surrendering, ("Sure, whatever sounds good to you"). But most often, my default was the worst move of them all, pretending nothing was wrong, ("No, I'm fine. Really, I'm FINE!").

Nick is more introverted than I am and prefers to spend time at home. I was (and still am) very social and liked going out with friends. It seemed to me that Nick never wanted to go out and I always wanted to go out. At that point in my life, I was unskilled in advocating for myself, and it never occurred to me that I could go out without him. My idea of being a couple meant doing everything together. When Nick declined plans, it felt as if I'd been sentenced to staying home, but I worried that calling out this difference in how we wanted to spend our time would damage our relationship. Instead of having a discussion about it, I nurtured the situation into a greater problem through avoidance, eventually growing resentful and bitter about all the activities I believed Nick was making me miss.

One night, soon after we began living together, my team had plans to go out after work. I asked Nick if he wanted to go. He told me he wasn't in the mood to go out with my colleagues. In all the time I'd spent building a wall of resentment around this issue, I'd become convinced that if I went without him, Nick would be upset about being left at home alone. In my mind, I'd just committed to living with someone who never wanted to go anywhere, which made me feel like I was committing to never going anywhere. I felt trapped.

"Fine," I said. Inside, I seethed. At twenty-five years old, my emotional regulation wasn't quite mature at that point. The anger from all the times I'd missed out on something I wanted to do began bubbling up. My flight response kicked into action, and I desperately wanted to remove myself from the situation to avoid conflict. I felt like I needed to get as far away from Nick as I could before I exploded.

"That's fine. I'm going to bed," I said, retreating. Of course, at that point, I was so wound up that the way I said "fine," made it perfectly clear that I wasn't fine.

Nick gave me a few moments to cool off, but then he came in and sat on the edge of the bed.

"Yeah, we can't do that," he said.

"I'm really tired," I told him, pulling the covers over my head.

"No, we need to talk about it. In this house we talk things through."

Oh, he was so right. And of course, when you're angry with someone, you don't want them to be right. I was trapped under the covers in a state of cognitive dissonance. I loved him, and I wanted our relationship to work, but having that conversation required vulnerability and swallowing my ego. I had to let go of all the self-righteous feelings that come with anger, and I had to admit that I felt differently than he did about going out.

I also knew that Nick was worth the discomfort of tackling this difficult conversation head-on. I pulled the blankets down under my chin, took a deep breath, and started to share how I felt and what I was struggling with.

Nick did the same.

A funny thing happened. While I had always feared that sharing how I felt would make a conflict worse, as Nick and I talked, we actually worked through the tension. Nick explained that he just doesn't enjoy going out in large groups with people he doesn't know well. He also told me that he didn't mind if I went out without him. He wouldn't feel left behind. Instead, he'd be happy to see me happy and also feel like I was sparing him an uncomfortable situation.

Since we were able to talk about it, over time, we worked out ways to enjoy social time together with friends at home or in small groups, and I learned to feel comfortable going out on my own. Even still, all these years later, when I go out with friends, Nick makes a point to say, "Have fun! Enjoy your time!" to remind me that he's happy for me to go out and have a good time with friends.

As discussion became our practice, we noticed that every time we had a conversation to work through a tension point, we became closer. Often it isn't the tension that creates the distance, but the toleration of that tension.

My journey of conflict avoidance recovery continued as I entered the workforce and began to witness firsthand the impact that conversations around conflict had, not only on the success of the team as a whole, but on the team members personally.

Learning Leadership

My first exposure to formal leadership development came when I had a summer job as a camp director and ropes course facilitator. I was a nineteen-year-old theatre major, leading groups of executives through various obstacles where communication and trust were key to successful completion. I worked with teams who not only excelled, but were also energized by the challenges. I also witnessed group situations where contempt hung in the air, choking everyone like bad perfume. I observed all the eye rolling, cutting sarcasm, blaming, and disconnecting that happen when a team's culture turns toxic.

After graduating with a degree in theatre performance and theatre education from the University of Northern Iowa, I applied for my first office job. Like any good person living in Des Moines, my first office job was in insurance. To say I was a square peg in a round insurance industry hole is an understatement.

During my interview, the hiring managers asked if I thought I could sit still in a cubicle. I told them I didn't know, but I was ready to find out!

I was not particularly interested in insurance. Mostly, I wanted to have good benefits and my nights free for theatre rehearsals. However, it was at this company that I discovered my love of training and directly learned the massive impact a leader could have on how someone saw themselves.

During this time, I went back to school and got my master's degree in leadership development at Drake University. Through my graduate studies, I truly fell in love with the philosophy and practices of Adaptive Leadership, a leadership framework developed by Harvard professors Ronald Heifetz, Alexander Grashow, and Marty Linsky that "helps individuals and organizations adapt and thrive in challenging environments." Through their work, I was introduced not only to the idea of the elephant in the room, but the understanding that truly adaptive cultures are ones where the elephant can be called out. Thus, a new curiosity was born. I wrote my master's thesis on Adaptive Leadership and began considering the question I've been working with for the last decade: how do you create a culture where the elephants can be addressed and better yet, prevented?

While I was learning about the tenets of what it takes to lead an adaptive culture, the organization where I worked was experiencing real changes and threats as the result of the 2008 financial crisis. I vividly recall receiving an email from senior leaders to all employees, informing us that due to financial strain, we would be exploring options for "reduction."

Reduction seems like such a benign term, doesn't it? It sounds calm and scientific, but the vague nature of this message sent everyone scrambling. As a team lead, my team members started sending me frantic emails and stopping by my desk to ask if I had additional information. I didn't. I had learned of the *reduction* at the same moment they had. I tried hard to keep my cool because not only did I not know what this meant for our team, but I also didn't know what reduction meant for me.

My colleague Janel and I went to talk with our director about the email.

"Are we going to talk about this?" we asked.

Pause.

"Talk about what?" she said and turned back to her computer.

It was clear that we were not going to have a conversation.

In the avoidance of even acknowledging the herd of elephants stomping across the floor, our trust in our director was trampled.

The questions from team members soon shifted from "What is going to happen to us?" to "Why won't they even acknowledge us?" and then "What are they hiding from us?"

This was a lynchpin moment for me. The situation illustrated so clearly that a void of information creates the perfect conditions for doubt to thrive. Clarity kills doubt, but sometimes clarity takes courage.

Looking back, I still don't agree with how the situation was handled, but I certainly understand why my director (who really was an amazing leader overall) chose that path. I can understand because I know that path well. The reality is that avoiding the hard stuff feels like the easier choice. However, in choosing to avoid, we're often making a choice to prioritize protection over courageous connection.

Easy Doesn't Always Mean Effective

In her seminal book *Daring Greatly: How the Courage to Be Vulnerable Transforms the Way We Live, Love, Parent, and Lead*, Brené Brown describes this moment of courageous connection through her definition of vulnerability: "Vulnerability sounds like truth and feels like courage. Truth and courage aren't always comfortable, but they're never weakness."

In *The Practice of Adaptive Leadership: Tools and Tactics for Changing Your Leadership and the World*, Ronald Heifetz, Marty Linsky, and Alexander Grashow say, "Leadership requires the engagement of what goes on both above and below the neck. Courage requires all of you: heart, mind, spirit, and guts. And skill requires learning new competencies, with your brain training your body to become proficient at new techniques..."

As my desire to dance in the land of courageous conversations increased, I realized that my skills did not match my will. Sometimes I was too blunt, and too passionate. Sometimes I couldn't control my emotions or didn't know how to respond when the other person couldn't control their emotions either. I grew frustrated when the other person became defensive, or I would be the defensive one, failing to recognize my own behavior as defense.

Little did I know that in one of the more difficult and unlikely times of my life, I would discover insight that created the foundation for how to show up more powerfully in conversations.

Wait...Why Are You Calling Them Elephants?

I have found that giving people language that's creative and playful can make it easier to take ownership of difficult situations. Lighthearted language does not mean the work is lightweight though. In using a well-known western metaphor, we also acknowledge that these behaviors are common. When we attach behaviors to shared language, we are able to correctly identify instead of accuse.

While a certain amount of heat is needed for transformation to occur in a relationship, too much heat can result in aggression or avoidance. Using creative language is a way for us to regulate the heat without turning it down so much that we stay inside our comfort zones. Focusing a conversation on elephants allows us to say, "Oh, I do that funny thing too!"

When I conduct retreats and seminars, one of my favorite things to hear is: "Wow, Sarah, I think we've got an elephant!" It means we have a shared adventure ahead that everyone is more prepared to take.

A NEW PERSPECTIVE

On March 3, 2013, I was getting a massage. Halfway through the massage, I remember thinking it was the best massage I'd ever had. Ten minutes later, out of nowhere, like a switch that got flipped, relentless panic hijacked my mind and body. My heart started racing. My hands shook, and then tremors took over every inch of my being. I felt like my neck was swelling shut, blocking my airways, making me dizzy and weak. *This is it. This is the big one*, I thought. *If you pass out, you die.*

I slid off the massage table and sat on the floor. It felt like I was slipping in and out of consciousness.

My massage therapist called paramedics. While we waited for them, I called Nick.

"I don't know what's wrong, but something happened," I told him, my voice filled with panic and tears, thinking this might be the last time I talk to him. "I don't know if I'm going to make it."

At the hospital, after a full workup of testing, the doctor came in.

"Good news is that your heart, head, and lungs all look good."

"That's a relief," I said with a sigh. "So what happened?"

"You have an overstimulated sympathetic nervous system."

"Ok," I said, trying to pretend that I knew what he was talking about.

"What does that mean again?" I asked.

"You just had a panic attack," he responded, very matter-of-fact.

I knew people who had experienced panic attacks, and I felt relieved. I remember thinking to myself *I can handle a panic attack*. Unfortunately, any relief I had in that moment was short lived. What started as one episode of panic turned into a daily experience of that feeling of impending doom (the hallmark of a panic attack). After three months in this new reality, I was diagnosed with panic disorder, which is defined as repeated episodes of panic and anxiety.

I tried to make it through my everyday life. At work, sometimes I'd experience aftershocks of panic, staring at my computer screen, trying to hold it together. I went home exhausted every single night. I was so disoriented. I constantly wished I didn't have to deal with panic anymore.

I began to work through the panic in therapy and by embracing mindfulness and meditation. In building a practice of observing, I was able to remind myself that the panic was temporary. Mindfulness—paying attention nonjudgmentally and giving grace to myself—became a lifesaver for me.

I learned to slow down and pay attention to things inside and outside of me that I hadn't before. It was such a transformation to set aside my judgment and fill those spaces with curiosity about the world and the people in it. This exercise in compassionate curiosity—born of my darkest moment—started me on my path to finding my calling.

You may be wondering how panic disorder relates to dealing with elephants in the room. As it turns out, some of the tactics used for treating panic also work on elephants. On my journey of finding relief from panic disorder, I learned mindfulness concepts like being present with your emotions and discomfort without judgment. I'd always been curious about the world around me, but my mindfulness practice helped me take my curiosity from external to internal, shifting focus from easy stuff to the hard stuff. Most importantly, this practice gave me the ability to be curious even during conflict and discomfort.

I also began researching the nervous system, which led me to a deeper understanding of how our brains work, and I became particularly fascinated by the ways our brains operate when under stress.

Combining this new knowledge with my coaching training gave me the tools, understanding, and compassion to show up powerfully and have conversations that matter. It was like a switch flipped, and I went all in.

Now I'm in the process of becoming a reformed conversation avoider. I'm passionate about having conversations that go below the surface into what I lovingly call the chewy nougat zone, where we strengthen our personal and professional relationships. As a leadership coach, researcher, and keynote speaker, my role is to create the space and safety for people to set their intentions, see their blind spots, have the conversations they're avoiding, and build trust through those interactions.

Through my work with thousands of teams and senior leaders across an array of industries, I've learned that chronic avoidance of important conversations is a cultural issue in many companies. This culture is best described as *violent politeness*, a term coined by Gianpiero Petriglieri, an associate professor of organizational behavior at INSEAD business school in Fontainebleau, France. Petriglieri describes violent politeness as "situations in which people in groups would rather bite their tongues than openly express their disagreements or misgivings." Small conflicts turn into major problems when we feed the elephant in the room by working around a barrier instead of talking about it.

Ed Catmull, former president of Pixar Animation and Walt Disney Studio Animation, with the help of Amy Wallace, summed up the cost of a violently polite culture best in their book *Creativity, Inc.*: "If there is more truth in the hallways than in meetings, you have a problem."

Through this book, I'll help you understand what the elephant in the room is, how it's affecting your relationships, and how employing curiosity and having conversations that matter can be the solution to getting that elephant out of your office and building trust back into your relationships.

How I Can Help You

Consider this book your personal workshop. I'm here to help. I'll teach you how to show up differently and acknowledge the elephants in the room through chronic curiosity, self-assessment, and reflection. We'll employ a Curiosity-First Approach and nurture a willingness to wade into difficult conversations. When we do, that elephant can move on, and trust can move in.

Through the course of these chapters, we'll discuss:

- What are the different types of elephants, what creates them, and how can we identify them?

- How to figure out if you're feeding the elephant, and why elephants get fed.

- How to talk about the elephant in the room without causing a stampede, using a Curiosity-First Approach.

- Why it's uncomfortable to have those elephant conversations.

- How to be someone your team members can come to with vulnerable issues.

- What to do when you encounter an elephant that feels like it can't be freed.

- What's possible for you and your team when an elephant is freed.

Remember, I'm a work in progress just like you. Conversations are difficult when we fear we stand to lose something. I still face conversations that require me to give myself a pep talk and take a few deep breaths to calm my beating heart before I can dive in.

But it's worth it! As we take this journey, remember to start small, give yourself grace, and practice extending that grace to others too. Heart work can be hard work.

Let's get started! Our growth as individuals and in relationships lives just beyond the comfort zone. But you are not alone. We are in this together.

Part 1

PACHYDERMS ON PARADE

1

Signs There Might Be an Elephant in the Room

When I first started my company, a manufacturing client hired me to do a workshop with their senior leadership team about receiving the information they'd gotten in their 360-degree feedback reports. The Human Resources specialist who hired me said, "I think there's an opportunity for us to strengthen trust. What can we do?"

Since I think it's always important to be up front about setting realistic expectations, I explained we weren't going to be able to do a full 180 in a three-hour morning workshop. Still, though, I said we could certainly work on making sure the team had some of the right tools to think differently about their work relationships and gain an understanding of how to create an environment of psychological safety.

Why is psychological safety so important?

25

Research shows that one of the things most high-performing teams have in common is a high level of psychological safety—something the giants have studied in great depth, including Google, which identified it as one of five factors of team success. It looks like this: in a psychologically safe environment, every member of a team can show up as themselves, take risks, make mistakes, ask for help, and even fail, while feeling valued. Creating an environment like this is vital to the success and health of an organization and is a strong step on the path to building trust.

After we explored the idea of psychological safety, I asked what I thought was a benign question. "What are some things you feel this team does well to create a psychologically safe environment?"

Crickets. There were twenty people on this team, but nobody said anything. I caught a few people side-eyeing each other, but otherwise, everyone looked away.

When I work with a group and no one answers a question, it could mean a number of things. It may mean they don't feel safe giving an answer, they don't feel comfortable speaking up in front of everyone, they don't understand the question, or it could be about something else entirely.

I took note of that silence and cleared up the possibility that they didn't understand the question by making sure we were working from a shared understanding of psychological safety. But I suspected the elephant would rear her head soon. When we took our first break, I caught a glimpse of a long gray trunk.

One of the team members sidled up to me and quietly said, "Yeah, it was interesting when you were talking about psychological safety. I think we struggle with that. I don't think that we have psychological safety."

When that team member left and I was about to leave the room, another person came up to me and said, "That's interesting. When you asked the question about psychological safety, and you didn't get a response—what does that mean? Does that mean we don't have psychological safety?"

I flipped the question back on her.

"Well, I don't know because I don't know your team," I said. "So, I think the important question is, what did that mean to you?"

"That we don't have psychological safety."

As everyone was coming back from break, a third person, a man who had not overheard either of these conversations, came over and said, "That was really interesting when nobody responded. I wasn't surprised."

The woman sitting next to me joined in, nodding in agreement.

We definitely had an elephant in the room, and when we suspect an elephant, we have a choice: to free or to feed our elephant.

My desire for comfort needed to be set aside for the team's need for my courage. I quickly asked my HR partner whether we should move forward with the workshop as planned or take a learning detour to get curious about the situation. She agreed that we should address the elephant.

As everyone returned from break and settled in, I said, "I want to share an observation. When I asked about psychological safety, there was silence, which made me wonder if there was some depth to the situation. Then over the break, I heard from a few people who mentioned that they weren't surprised by the lack of candor. I'm curious, as you hear me share this observation, what comes up for you?"

At first, it was quiet again, but I held steady and waited. Eventually, people started to share in ways they hadn't through the first section of the workshop. They really opened up, and it turned into a beautiful conversation.

We explored how the founder had passed away two years prior. Some of the people on the team knew him, but many didn't. Team members who hadn't been with the company long struggled with the idea of holding up the founder's legacy when they didn't know who he was. What we uncovered is that a large portion of the team felt uncertain about their role in the organization, and by acknowledging this elephant, we were able to open up space for a powerful and constructive conversation.

Before the end of our workshop, we debriefed on what allowed us to have that open conversation so we could create a list of specific practices the team could use to address elephants in the future. We'll discuss ways to talk about the elephant in Chapter 4, but I wanted to share what they identified as practices that worked for them:

- Explore the topic without the need for a solution.

- Allow time to talk about the team and not just about tasks.

- Have courage to ask and receive hard questions.

- See the bigger picture.

- Make sure everyone is heard.

FOOTPRINTS AND BROKEN BRANCHES

The elephant in the room can wreak havoc while everyone does their best to look away. Unlike an elephant you'd spot on safari, relationship elephants don't leave a physical trail of footprints and broken branches, but they do leave a psychological trail. The good news is there are solid clues we can use to track and expose these elephants.

- People become quiet.

- Team members exchange knowing glances (or alternatively, eye contact ceases and everyone seems suddenly interested in their notes).

- Someone poses a question, but nobody answers (or alternatively, people respond with sarcasm or passive aggression).

- People shift in their seats, fidget, or change the subject.

- People's body language is closed off (i.e., crossed arms).

- Team members have meetings after the meeting or side chats.

What Are "Meetings After the Meetings?"

A meeting after the meeting is the most obvious sign that there's an elephant in the room and an important one to pay attention to. I'm sure you've experienced this before: after the meeting is called to a close, the conversation continues but not with the people who need to be included. A meeting happening after the meeting doesn't have to be another gathering in a conference room. It can be as simple as two team members walking out of a weekly conference whispering some form of "Oh, my! Can you believe Jane acted that way?" That kind of discussion could just mean these people are gossiping, but it could also be a sign that they didn't feel safe, empowered, or have the skills to address an elephant.

Post-meeting discussion is the primary way elephants get revealed to me when I run retreats and workshops. On a break, someone from the team I'm working with will pull me aside to talk about an issue. I can always tell it's coming, from the look of concern on their face, and their hushed voice as they ask, "Are you going to discuss X?" or "When in the day would be a good time for me to bring X up?" This is a clear sign we have an elephant, and as soon as we reconvene, we need to find it and free that baby!

How Does It Feel to Have an Elephant in the Room?

Sometimes we've gotten so good at tolerating an elephant that we don't realize it's there. Or we don't allow ourselves to fully register the presence of an elephant because it's too scary or uncomfortable. If we numb our intuitive senses, the elephant can quickly become the norm. It's helpful to figure out what the presence of an elephant feels like so we can begin to connect those warning signs with the need to take action.

For me, an elephant in the room often comes across as an energy of direct, silent heaviness. There's tension, and I feel tightness and pressure that can make it hard to breathe—almost as if an elephant were sitting on my chest. My eyes dart back and forth, looking for the cause. I'll think *Oh shit. What's going on here?*

When I'm facilitating a workshop, and it's not my elephant, I will still feel the pressure and anxiety; my heart will race, but I also get excited because I know this team has the potential for a powerful learning moment.

Here's how other people in an online survey[1] have described feeling when there's an elephant in the room:

- "Tense, awkward, impending doom until someone addresses the elephant."

---

1 Digital and social media survey conducted 7/11/19

- "Tingling on skin, heart racing, irritation."

- "Unease, uncertainty, exasperation (just talk about it already!) wondering if it's my place to speak up and address it."

- "A bit of fear. Loss of control. A sense of 'if we can't talk about it, my job here is much more difficult, if not impossible.' Will I be shunned if I call it out?"

- "It's uncomfortable. You feel as if you want to speak out but aren't sure if you should or not."

- "Depending on my relationship with the elephant (and I've been on all sides of the great beast), I can actually experience physical symptoms such as tingling, sweating, righteous anger, defensiveness for the elephant or others, my thoughts can begin racing, I can feel the desire to escape if my security is threatened. Every possible emotion except joy or confidence can show up."

- "Anxiousness, nervousness, urge to fidget, sense of release when I'm out of the situation or know it's never going to be addressed."

- "Anxiety, sadness, at times lonely, anger, fear, frustration."

- "A little uneasy and nervous. I am a people pleaser, so I want to make people feel better or avoid an 'explosion' of negative emotions."

- "It's uncomfortable with a sense of no trust because people can't or won't be open and honest—often because they feel they might hurt someone's feelings."

- "Sometimes hopelessness. Internal dialogue—do I go through this again or just keep quiet. Can I approach this another way? Not sure that I have paid close enough attention to my physical reaction, but there must be some tension there."

- "It depends on the group. If it is a group or team I am comfortable with, I will make a joke or try to blow off whatever caused the situation in the first place."

- "Curious."

- "Mirth generally. It shouldn't be an issue for adults to address them so it usually makes me laugh."

- "Dread in the pit of my stomach, tightened throat, fighting off frowning, narrowing my eyes."

- "Almost like a fog that tightens your chest."

The most common words used from the data we collected were: tense, anxious, and awkward.

Take a moment and think about your own experience. What does it feel like to you when you are experiencing an elephant in the room?

What Creates an Elephant?

Often, I will hear people speak about the elephant in the room as if it is a person—but it's not. A person, process, or project may cause issues, but it is our avoidance that ultimately creates the elephant. Your annoying coworker is not an elephant. Your coworker's annoying behavior is not even necessarily the elephant. But your aversion to addressing your coworker's annoying behavior could be what gives the elephant life—that is, if that aversion prevents you from productively collaborating with him on the project.

> This is where we are really trying to drill home: the elephant is the avoidance. The elephant in the room is created when people see a topic, problem, or risk that impacts success, but they avoid acknowledging it, do not attempt resolution, or assume a resolution isn't possible.

Conflicts and disagreements on their own don't equal an elephant in the room. Sometimes we may overcome our avoidance and still not be able to resolve the conflict. There's a common limiting belief that a positive relationship doesn't have a lot of conflict, but a productive relationship is one where all parties can disagree openly, effectively, and respectfully. Those relationships recover quickly from disagreement and don't linger in a conflicted state. Relationships where disagreement is well managed are elephant-free, or at the very least, don't encourage elephants to stick around for long. In effective relationships, all parties expect a fair and timely cycle of disagreement to recovery, making it easier to delve into necessary conflicts from a point of psychological safety.

Unlike conflict in an effective relationship, conflict in a relationship where elephants are present will likely lead to resentment, paralysis, or a feeling of resignation. When we don't recover, repair, and move on more powerfully from disagreements, conflict becomes a barrier to success, and the elephant search needs to begin.

Acceptance vs. Resignation

It's important for us to define resignation as separate from acceptance as we continue our discussion of elephants. A healthy disagreement isn't a competition of who is right, but rather it is a commitment to learning as much as we can. That said, in any relationship, there are always going to be moments of loss and disagreements simply because we all hold different values, perspectives, experiences, and opinions. How we show up in those moments of difference can have significant impact on how we think, feel, and act.

Resignation literally means to give up. Resignation is a reaction.

Think of resignation as "Well, it is what it is."

Acceptance, on the other hand, is the act of taking something that is offered. Acceptance is a response.

Think of acceptance as "Ok, that's what we have to work with."

You can feel the difference between the two. Resignation is to admit defeat. Acceptance is acknowledging what has happened.

Resignation is toleration. Acceptance allows us the possibility to move forward or move on.

The High Cost of Elephant Upkeep

An elephant left to roam free in a workplace can cause a lot of damage to the organization but more importantly, to the people involved. Some of that damage can be immediately apparent, but some you may never see. Think of an apple with its skin on. It looks like a normal apple. Now, imagine that you've dropped that apple a few times or it got crushed in your grocery bag. When you select that apple, it may still look fine, but it isn't until you cut it open that you will see the bruising and damage. The same is true when we allow conflict to fester—even if that conflict is merely imagined and lives in our own heads.

Here is what happens when we allow an elephant to linger:

- Distrust increases and trust decreases.

- Team members grow disengaged and disheartened.

- Creativity and innovation can't thrive.

- People spend energy actively avoiding instead of taking action.

- Ongoing stress can harm a person's mental and physical health.

This list is not comprehensive. In fact, one of the most simple, direct costs of not freeing an elephant is loss of time. Let's take a closer look: years ago, I worked with a team member, Adriana, who had received feedback from her manager that surprised her. She felt like her manager was questioning her intelligence. I knew Adriana's manager, and it seemed out of character for him to share the kind of feedback she brought to me. While I didn't think the situation was a big deal, it felt like a big deal to Adriana. The size of the elephant is in the eye of the beholder. A situation that might not seem worth worrying about to you may feel overwhelming to the other person.

Though she needed to have a conversation to clarify and free that elephant that was her avoidance, it took a month for Adriana to take that leap. When I asked her how much time she thought she spent on this situation, she figured about twenty hours total just *thinking* about the problem and the impending conversation.

Yes! Twenty hours.

As you might imagine, the beautiful ending to this story is that the conversation clarified the confusion. Adriana left feeling even better about herself and her relationship with her manager. Not only did Adriana understand her manager's feedback more effectively, but he also learned how to clarify his feedback for aligned impact. She also realized she had the courage to approach a sensitive conversation, and he had the courage to engage with her.

According to data collected by Cy Wakeman for her book *Reality-Based Leadership*, people spend on average six hours a day dealing with drama. That means freeing an elephant can have an enormous positive impact on productivity. Adriana's story is just one example of how this can look in the real world.

The other side of this scenario could have been that Adriana did not have enough trust in her situation or feel enough psychological safety to approach having the conversation with her manager. Power dynamics are heavy at play in our world today, especially at work, whether you realize them or not. Power dynamics show up along the hierarchy of roles, representation or underrepresentation within a group, culture, and policies of the company, among others. Sometimes the risk for speaking up may have real consequences to our livelihoods, both personally and professionally. While my goal is for you to feel more confident freeing elephants, the truth is that *you* decide if you feel safe enough to free an elephant. There is no shame in keeping one around awhile longer until you feel safe. And the truth is, there may be times where you'll never be safe.

The Power of Trust

Key to successfully overcoming the avoidance and freeing an elephant is the trust component of psychological safety. And look, leaders: I hear you, and I trust you when you say you're good, kind, and understanding. As we've seen in the story above and will see time and time again in this book, even those of us who are kind and wonderful may have people in our sphere who don't feel safe sharing feedback with us. We can influence someone's feelings of trust, but ultimately, we don't get to decide how trustworthy we are.

> **This is important, so let me say it again:** You don't get to decide if you're trustworthy. Other people do.

And the reality is if people don't trust you, they're likely not going to tell you they don't, even when you ask. So how can we build a culture of safety and trust, especially related to hard conversations? One way is through feedback, which we'll explore later in this book. For now, internalize this: you can say you're open to hearing feedback, and that may be true. But hearing something and getting curious about it, internalizing it, and doing something about it are two very different things. The latter is required to build the psychological safety you want—and that all the Adrianas out there need and deserve.

What's Next?

Not all elephants are the same size. Your coworker could be heading into an interview with broccoli in their teeth, and you and your team members see it but don't say anything. That not saying anything is a micro-elephant. On the opposite extreme is the gigantic, mastodon-sized elephant sitting on a company as they struggle with a truly toxic culture and a CEO who is unwilling to address the damage and/or their role in the toxicity.

Often, we lean on our avoidance because we're trying to protect our relationships or ourselves. These are natural reactions. When we feel stressed, our brains feel threatened, and they go into protection mode. How does this work, and how can we use this information about how our brain processes events on our journey to face and overcome our elephants? We'll discuss in the next chapter.

Get Curious

- Think of a time when you've experienced or observed an elephant in the room. What behaviors did you notice in yourself and others?

- What does it feel like physically to you when you notice an elephant is in the room?

- When you think about having a conversation about a conflict, what makes you feel unsafe? What makes you feel safe?

2

This Is What Your Brain Is Doing on Stress

Imagine getting an email from your boss that says only: "Hey, stop by my office when you get a chance. We need to have a quick chat."

Does just reading that give you "the spins" a little?

I'm going to go ahead and assume that in that scenario, your first thought wouldn't be that you were getting a raise or a promotion, right? That's not how most brains work. The most common jump in that scenario is to *Oh no, what did I do?* followed by a mental scan of how you might have screwed up recently.

Did you think you were alone in experiencing frantic feelings over a "We need to talk" email?

(You're not.)

Did you think it means you're too negative or too anxious?

(It doesn't.)

How Do You Feel When an Elephant Hangs Around?

I asked over three hundred survey participants a question: What did they feel when there was an elephant in the room that wasn't being freed?

With one exception*, the responses fell into three categories:

- **Tension**—The language around tension included the following: "A fog that is tight around the chest, shoulders tight, sick to the stomach, I was so nervous through the whole meeting."

- **Anxiety**—Respondents felt heavy and anxious. There was discomfort from feelings of uncertainty about how people would respond or what would happen afterward.

- **Fear**—Respondents included questions like: "Will I be shunned for speaking up? Will there be retaliation? Will I hurt someone? Will I be hurt if we can't talk about it?"

*That one person responded by writing, "I felt curious to see what we would do with it." (I don't know who wrote this, but I want to be you when I grow up!)

There is a specific part of the brain to thank for that sinking "Oh, shit," feeling. It's called the amygdala, and it's my favorite because amygdala activity is one of the most significant clues to why we do what we do under stress.

If you want to build powerful partnerships at work and at home, it will serve you to understand a bit of behavioral science, psychology, and biology that comes with being human. We all have protective behaviors built into our fundamental nature that create resistance to conflict and discomfort. Those protective behaviors are also what triggers us to feed an elephant. We've survived and evolved as a species because these protective behaviors have compelled us to lifesaving avoidant or aggressive actions. But our innate survival tendencies often make it harder to handle issues that aren't actually life and death, even though they might feel like it.

Brain chemistry, instinct, and behavior are complex subjects, and I'm going to highlight some of the mindsets, questions, and tools that can help you gain a better understanding of yourself, the people around you, and why it can be so hard to free elephants.

I LOVE MY AMYGDALA

The amygdala sits at the base of your brain and is considered part of what scientists call our primitive brain. The amygdala plays a significant role in instantaneous shifts from calm to fearful. The amygdala's job is to save your life. If you cross the street and a car is coming at you, your amygdala sparks a chain of reactions to get you to move the hell out of the way. However, the amygdala isn't just scanning the environment for physical threats; it also responds to emotional threats and harm to our ego. Like being excluded from a group or being disrespected.

Unfortunately, our survival mechanisms haven't caught up with the increase in physical safety that we've established through our evolution and that most of us are lucky enough to experience. Our brains and bodies still react to threats with the same intensity as our ancestors experienced when they had to run from a bear or a saber-toothed tiger. This is why we feel like we're being chased by a bear when our boss sends a "We need to talk" email. The jolt we get from our body is a response to the possibility of a threat, and your amygdala isn't all that interested in figuring out the difference between your boss and a snarling grizzly.

I like to compare the amygdala to my tiny, shaky, neurotic Chihuahua, Seymour. Seymour sleeps with his ears in full radar position so he can pay attention to the environment and jump into action the instant anything seems out of place. When you're startled by a sound, your amygdala is a lot like Seymour barking at our mailperson with an intensity that feels like he's shouting, "What the hell was that? Why are you at my house? What are you dropping in the mailbox?"

Since your amygdala's job is to spur you toward instant, lifesaving action, your first thoughts about that email from your boss will not be rational. Stirred-up feelings trigger cascading reactions. Your imagination rockets to ideas of being fired. Your heart is racing, and your palms are sweaty. You feel fidgety and sick to your stomach. You have the sense these feelings are trying to tell you something important, even though all you know for sure is that your amygdala was triggered by an email, and now you feel like Seymour getting upset about the mailperson.

Some amygdalae are more reactive than others. Still, we all have a little brain-Chihuahua sitting in a lighthouse, continually scanning for threats, ready to call our body into action the minute it perceives a threat. This means everyone you know has most likely also felt that primal panic feeling before. You are not alone.

Amy G. Dala

My interest in the sympathetic nervous system began when I ended up in the hospital with heart palpations, difficulty breathing, and an undeniable sense that I was about to die. As you know from the Introduction, after running a full panel of tests, the doctor diagnosed me with an overstimulated sympathetic nervous system.

The doctor gave me a basic explanation, but after experiencing the full power of the sympathetic nervous system, I needed to do my own research to understand what was going on with my brain.

A panic attack is literally a triggered sense of impending doom, caused by the amygdala. Studying this process made me keenly aware of the ways smaller triggers and smaller reactions happen regularly in our interactions with each other.

When your amygdala is triggered (which can happen in as little as .07 seconds), you aren't able to think innovatively or creatively, and you're also not able to build trust. Your amygdala has important jobs, but building trust isn't one. By making intentional efforts to deregulate adrenaline and cortisol (stress hormones), and nurture interactions that increase oxytocin (a soothing hormone in the parasympathetic process), we can improve our connections with other people. Learning to be kind and empathetic to the amygdalae in our midst (including our own) holds the key to having brave conversations, freeing elephants, and building powerful relationships.

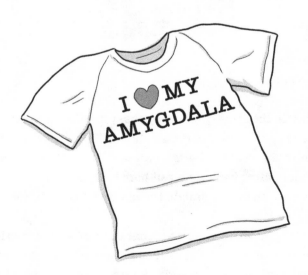

To embrace the incredible power of my amygdala, I had a friend design a T-shirt for me that reads, I HEART MY AMYGDALA. It's an awesome shirt, but the positioning of the letters confused people. Whenever I wore it, someone would inevitably say, "That's a great shirt. Who's Amy G. Dala? Is she a singer? Is that a band?"

While working with a leadership team, I told them my shirt story as we discussed how being mindful of amygdala reactivity can improve relationships. One of the team members reported back a few months later to say that they decided to include Amy G. Dala on the participant list for senior meetings, as a reminder be kind to everyone's amygdalae.

Food for Thought:
Feedback Feels Personal to Amy G.

Are you searching for the quickest way to spend some time with your Amy G. Dala or someone else's? The answer is simple: feedback.

One of the things I hear a lot is, "I wish people didn't take feedback so personally. How do I give feedback so people don't get defensive?"

Sometimes you can't give feedback without triggering someone's amygdala (or accept feedback without having yours triggered) because the reaction happens so quickly.

Now that you know, your goal for feedback shouldn't be to get rid of that initial reaction. Rather, it should be to maintain your awareness and help yourself and those around you gain their awareness so you can improve recovery time.

We cannot always stop the reaction. But we can notice, name, and redirect the reaction.

The Sympathetic vs. Parasympathetic Nervous Systems

When your amygdala is hijacked—a term first mentioned in Daniel Goleman's 1995 book *Emotional Intelligence*—it is overwhelming. Some psychologists call it "being flooded." What happens when your car engine gets flooded?

Right. It all shuts down.

That's because the amygdala sends signals to our bodies to produce adrenaline and cortisol. Then, we can lose access to the functions of the prefrontal lobe (which allows us to access such tools as logic, reasoning, and listening).

In short, we're in a survival state. We're hyper-focused.

For example, say you smell something burning in the kitchen. Before you're even fully conscious of the smell, the amygdala fires off a "Danger, Will Robinson!" message to the hypothalamus. Your hypothalamus acts as command central for the rest of the body, channeling the word about that burning smell to the sympathetic nervous system, which acts as a rocket launcher, shooting adrenaline through your system. Adrenaline pushes blood through our veins, causing our heart to race. Our breathing rate increases so we can take in extra oxygen to wake our brains for alert survival response, cutting off access to the higher-functioning parts of our mind, allowing us to focus only on survival. Stored sugar and fat are released for a boost of energy. You run as fast as you can toward the kitchen, prepared to fight for your life.

After you discover the smell was merely the toast your spouse accidentally charred, your soothing, parasympathetic system can restore access to the higher-functioning parts of your brain. You're now able to register that the threat to your home and safety is nil, but that adrenaline and cortisol are still there.

Ways to Calm the Amygdala

Some powerful ways to calm down the amygdala response by activating the parasympathetic nervous system are:

- **Notice and name**. The act of noticing our amygdala has been triggered can quickly start to slow down the reaction. It will not remove the trigger, but to acknowledge internally or externally that "I've been triggered" is a powerful start to disrupt the stress response.

- **Take a breath**. Our breath is always with us and always in our control. Breathing in for four counts, holding for four counts, and then breathing out for four counts will massage our vagus nerve and supply more oxygen to our brains.

- **Take a break**. Give our body time to metabolize the adrenaline and cortisol. A break could include going for a walk. Moving helps our body switch to a more relaxed state. Note that it can take about an hour to metabolize adrenaline and up to twenty-four hours to metabolize excessive amounts of cortisol.

We have a greater understanding and sensitivity around this reaction when the trigger is something physical, like the smell of smoke, or a near miss collision on the highway. But when it comes to emotional triggers, sometimes we find it hard to be patient with others or ourselves. We can feel ashamed by our reaction "over nothing," even though it makes sense that our survival response is triggered around fears of rejection. Acceptance in a tribe was once an urgent survival need and is still vital to our well-being.

Our sympathetic nervous system is truly spectacular. When we're in a fight for our lives, our brains and bodies have considerable ability to help us protect ourselves. If you've ever read a story about someone who lifts a car to save a family member trapped underneath, that's because their sympathetic nervous system allowed them to focus every ounce of energy available to them.

STRESS RESPONSES

Stress responses serve us well when they initiate self-protection in response to actual threats. When over-triggered in non emergency situations without self-management efforts, stress responses can become unhealthy, creating barriers and conflict and letting elephants in. They aren't inherently bad, but it's important to recognize when stress responses cross the line into unhelpful.

There are five major stress responses. We'll examine them together.

Fight

The fight stress response inspires aggressive or defensive action. Healthy fight behaviors include being assertive, setting boundaries, and protecting yourself or others when necessary. Unhealthy fight behaviors include active or passive aggression, blaming, or controlling. When you're in fight response, you might notice your voice is raised and you are speaking more quickly than normal.

Flight

The flight stress response inspires a desire to escape—and not always in a physical sense. If someone brings up a tense topic in a meeting and everyone is suddenly interested in their notes, that's a flight response in action. Healthy flight behaviors include engaging in busywork or hobbies and removing yourself from toxic situations. Unhealthy flight behaviors include catering to your perfectionist tendencies, over-worrying, or trying to escape problems that need resolution. When you're in flight response, you might notice yourself changing the subject in difficult conversations or distracting yourself to avoid interaction.

Freeze

The freeze stress response inspires us to shut down, plain and simple. Healthy freeze behaviors include recognizing when a struggle isn't productive and being patient enough to take pertinent action later rather than instantaneously, when emotions may be high. Unhealthy freeze behaviors include not standing up for others or mental paralysis. When you're in freeze response, you may notice an uptick in your absences or an overall decrease in the frequency or quality of your interactions with others.

Fawn

The fawn stress response compels us to do whatever we can to appease others in an attempt to remove their stress response. This comes from a place of protection, not altruism, and there's similarity between being helpful/keeping the peace and fawning. The difference lies in the motivation: Am I helping you to be helpful? Or am I helping you because I'm worried not doing it will trigger you? Healthy fawn behaviors include listening, compromising, and helping. Unhealthy fawn reposes include giving up your own needs and rights, harboring resentment for always giving in, and having a low sense of self. When you're in fawn response, you might notice a high degree of agreeableness and fear of triggering negative responses in others.

Flock

The flock stress response is when we seek out others to help us make meaning of the stressing event—that is, to try to understand how we should act or to validate our response. Flocking is what is often behind the "meetings after the meetings" or the "side eye" behaviors that come up when a challenge or barrier starts to emerge in meetings, for example. Healthy flock responses include reaching out to others to help us make sense of situations or to help us navigate how to respond appropriately. Unhealthy flock responses can happen when we only seek out those who agree with our point of view or talk to everyone but the person we should be talking to. While this is the last one on the list, it's often the first place we start when experiencing a stress response.

OTHER NORMAL
HUMAN REACTIONS

Now that we've discussed some physiological responses to stress, let's talk about the psychological side.

What does our brain do, whether we realize it or not? And what is so important to understand about these reactions when dealing with elephants? Let's take a look.

A Bias Toward the Negative

I receive feedback on every presentation or workshop I deliver. While often the feedback is very positive or helpful, there are times when comments can feel sharp or sting. I'm human, after all. Even if ninety-eight comments are positive, my brain will focus on the two that are hypercritical. Sound familiar? Even though I understand the brain on feedback and have helped hundreds of people learn to process feedback, those negative comments trigger my amygdala and light up my stress hormones. It is like a train I can't slow down until it reaches the end of the track. My brain commits them to memory as if the feedback was a threat, and it would serve me to remember every detail.

Receiving feedback effectively is a different animal—and one we'll spend much more time getting to know later in this book, beginning in Chapter 9.

Does this ever happen to you? You get feedback from others, and regardless of all the good things they say, you hyper-focus in on the negative ones? Congratulations. You are human.

We are far more likely to retain the negative moments than the positive. From a survival perspective, it makes sense. If you were out foraging for berries and encountered an angry bear, being able to remember the location of the encounter, the dimensions of the bear, and the tree you climbed to escape could serve you well in future berry collection efforts.

This is why we can pan through ninety-nine glowing five-star comments, looking for a one-star. In moments where you notice this behavior, it also helps to be aware that your brain may try to neutralize the threat by discrediting it. An easy way for the brain to build itself up again is to tear someone else down. Again, this behavior can happen so fast we aren't conscious we are even doing it. We all know that when it comes to building strong relationships and creating powerful impact, feedback is necessary. It's important to check yourself for discrediting behaviors that can be a detriment to your relationships.

Cognitive Dissonance

Years ago, my former boss and I were preparing to do a team intervention. As this was one of my first big challenges, I wanted to make sure we were being as thorough in approach as possible. My inner researcher welled up as we began to prepare our approach.

"Before we start this work, let's spend some time identifying and understanding what biases we're bringing into this project."

My boss said, "Oh no, Sarah. I pride myself on not having biases."

I didn't know where to begin. We all have biases. Some we may be aware of and many more we simply aren't. I could easily list off seven biases I'd seen both of us encounter in the past week and an additional five of my own, but she was completely unaware of the idea that she could exhibit bias at all (at least at this moment).

"We are all capable of believing things which we know to be untrue, and then, when we are finally proved wrong, impudently twisting the facts so as to show that we were right. Intellectually, it is possible to carry on this process for an indefinite time: the only check on it is that sooner or later a false belief bumps up against solid reality, usually on a battlefield."

–George Orwell, 1946

Why is it so difficult for us to see that our impact is different than what we intended?

It's not because you're a terrible person. It's a protection mechanism in our brain described as cognitive dissonance. Since my boss held the idea that being without bias was a possible and preferred trait, and defined herself as someone without bias, she was naturally avoidant of any discussion that might prove her sense of self wrong.

We experience cognitive dissonance when presented with information that is different from the beliefs we hold about ourselves and the world. Cognitive dissonance causes actual physical discomfort and may compel self-justification, denial, and the spreading of untruths. If we believe ourselves to be good people, but do bad things, we will seek ways to resolve this dissonance. Our resolutions can result in behaviors that are uniquely destructive to ourselves and others.

Cognitive dissonance is the natural enemy of curiosity. The instinct to protect ourselves from cognitive dissonance can make it hard to have vulnerable conversations and be open to hearing perspectives from others.

> "Most of us find it difficult if not impossible to say 'I was wrong, I made a terrible mistake.' This is why self-justification is more powerful and more dangerous than an explicit lie. It allows people to convince themselves that what they did was the best they could have done. And when we cross these lines we're justifying behavior that we know is wrong precisely so that we can continue to see ourselves as honest people and not as criminals or thieves."
>
> —Carol Tavris and Elliot Aronson, *Mistakes Were Made (But Not by Me): Why We Justify Foolish Beliefs, Bad Decisions, and Hurtful Acts*

Most people, when directly confronted by evidence that they were wrong, do not always change their point of view or plan of action but justify it even more tenaciously. We need to be aware that this tendency exists in all of us. Sometimes I can see it, but other times it takes people helping me see it.

Like most behaviors, the avoidance of cognitive dissonance happens in varying degrees with varied consequence. Avoidance of cognitive dissonance explains why you can justify eating a few grapes while you shop in the produce aisle, why the opposing team is always getting more favor from the referees, or—even more significantly—why a white person might believe they could never be racist because they "don't see color."

What Are
Shadow Intentions?

Though we're often walking around with good intentions, there's another side to the story: shadow intentions. Shadow intentions are our unconscious, potentially uncomfortable behaviors that come from a place of self-protection. Sometimes, our shadow intentions will show up as violent politeness, passive aggression, guilt-tripping, and more. This is a concept we'll unpack deeper as we move through this book.

WHAT'S NEXT?

Again, I want to remind you that all of these responses and behaviors are normal! They're part of the human experience. You're not a bad person if you feel panicked by feedback or want to flee the room when someone plunges into an uncomfortable conversation, if you only remember the negative feedback, or you eat grapes at the grocery store (but maybe stop that).

Remember that when you have self-protective reactions, it's because you might feel (or be) threatened, the issue at hand matters, and/or the relationships involved are important. It would be weird to be numb about the things that matter.

I want you to feel a little heat and discomfort over the role you're playing in feeding an elephant, though. You should take a step back to say, "Oh, wow. I'm handing over peanuts like crazy!" and then take responsibility for your part in the damage that may have been caused to your team and relationships. At the same time, I want you to remember that you're not flawed. You are not broken. It makes sense that it's uncomfortable to have a heated conversation with somebody. It makes sense that it can feel easier to be judgmental than to give someone the benefit of the doubt. Those high-emotion moments are your opportunity to determine the difference between the behaviors that make sense to your primal nervous system and what's actually productive in your long-term well-being and relationships. Powerful partnerships are rarely built in the land of protection. Rather, they are built in the land of transparency, authenticity, and empathy.

I also hope that this awareness can help you approach situations with empathy when you recognize these responses in other people. They probably aren't being difficult for the sake of being difficult. Instead, they are humans wired for protection who feel threatened. Their beautiful brains are simply doing what they do. That isn't to say there shouldn't be accountability in these moments, but there can also be a little more understanding. Now that you know you can move from reaction to response.

Seeing the elephant and understanding how it got there is the first step. There's power in saying, "I think we might have an elephant. Here's what I'm noticing..." But there's even more power in being able to identify the types of elephants intruding in your relationships. In the next chapter, we're going to get into the taxonomy of elephants and give you names to help you free the elephants in your world.

Get Curious

- Think of a time when your amygdala hijacked your brain. What did you think, feel, and do?

- When was a time your self-protection served you? When did it not?

- What can be a cue for you when you might be in the land of cognitive dissonance?

3

Naming Your Elephants

You can see the giant footprints all over the floor. The conference room feels like a swirling mess of misunderstanding and peanut shells. Something on your team is going very wrong, but you don't know what to fix because you're not sure exactly what's causing the problem.

Maybe you suspect you have an elephant, but you're scared to look for it.

We have a tendency to spend most of our days on autopilot, reacting from a place of habit instead of responding intentionally. We avoid seeing elephants out of an adherence to cultural norms, because of how we were raised, past traumatic experiences, self-protection, or the climate in our organization. Sometimes, we ignore elephants because we're moving so fast and think if we just keep up the pace, that elephant won't catch up with us. Or that things might just spontaneously improve. We've learned to tolerate these elephants and coexist with them. We assume this is the only way to navigate them. However, those elephants have a way of showing themselves at critical moments and creating big problems. Our work culture and our productivity improve if we do the work of noticing and naming out elephants.

We can't change something we don't notice and acknowledge, so the first step to freeing an elephant is admitting you have one. The next step is working to see it clearly.

Let's talk about why these elephants exist, their taxonomy, and what makes them stick around.

AVOIDING: SEEKING OUT
THE AVOIDEPHANT

When we avoid action in an attempt to remove the internal stress of a situation, an "Avoidephant" is created.

Avoidephants are our archetype—the basis from which all the future elephant species we'll discuss in this book have derived. An

Avoidephant pushes itself in the way of anyone trying to initiate a necessary conversation and keeps team members from clarifying important information.

The Avoidephant
(a·void'·eh·fent)

In the presence of an Avoidephant, we literally avoid conversations, opting to internalize our thoughts, feelings, and insights. Sometimes we even avoid the conversation with ourselves. The Avoidephant feeds on the fears of a team and the desire for safety and harmony. When an Avoidephant is allowed to stay in a room, it grows rapidly.

An Avoidephant Case Study

Michael was a CEO who genuinely cared for his team, yet Michael's team often felt that he didn't have their back, valuing his relationship with the board over his relationship with them. When Michael brought in board-suggested initiatives and asked for feedback, the team would often agree with his ideas or go silent. Michael knew that since his team would be responsible for enacting the initiatives, their ideas would be valuable. He thought they weren't always interested in the discussions, which felt frustrating at times.

When I met with his team to understand what was going on, I learned that they didn't feel empowered to speak against the board's initiatives because of the nature of the relationship Michael had with them. They genuinely liked Michael, and despite this issue, they knew he was a good guy, so they held hesitancy around the possibility of hurting his feelings. Michael valued his team and believed in their potential. He avoided bringing up his disappointment in their engagement because he feared it would damage morale. Violent politeness in action.

By feeding the Avoidephant, frustration built up on both sides. The team felt forced to implement initiatives that impacted their day-to-day work, which hurt their collaboration, created resentment toward Michael, and strained trust. When we dove in and had that difficult conversation, he hadn't realized they felt he wasn't on their side. Michael was able to hear what his team needed and was able to tell his team about the ways he tried to have their back with the board. It was a simple, albeit uncomfortable, conversation with a huge impact. Reassured of their relationship, the team shared their thoughts on the new initiatives with candor and freed the Avoidephant.

What You Might Hear if the Avoidephant Is in the Room

The language around the Avoidephant tends to be minimizing. To correctly identify the Avoidephant, listen for phrases like:

- "I know they're a good person..."

- "It's not that big of a deal anyway."

- "I don't want to make them feel bad."

- "I'm not going to give them feedback because they'll get defensive and take it out on me."

Questions to Ask if You or Someone Else May Be Feeding the Avoidephant*

- What's holding me back from having a transformative conversation?

- What am I afraid of when I imagine the conversation? Retaliation, exclusion, loss of harmony, hurt feelings, or something else?

- What confirms this fear?

- What disconfirms this fear?

In the case of the Avoidephant, remember, you may need to find allies who are willing to support you in speaking up. There is greater safety in numbers, but sometimes we have to be willing to speak and stand with courage alone.

IMAGINING:
TESTING THE IMAGIPHANT

Someone sends you a request by email, but they don't say "please" or "thank you," only "Hey, can you do this?" The story you tell yourself is that they're rude, or they're angry with you. Instead of considering that their email may have been written at a rushed moment or even with consideration for your efficiency, you get upset by the abrupt tone and hold on to that frustration. The act of holding frustration without an effort to clarify is what summons the Imagiphant.

The Imagiphant species of Avoidephants are born from stories you've told yourself and assumptions you've made without confirming or testing your beliefs. If you think you have an Imagiphant in your presence, it's important to remember that all of our perspectives influence our experiences, and our experiences influence our perspectives. Although the feelings you're having may not be based on the truth, it doesn't make it less real for you because it's your truth. When you lock yourself into one perspective about a situation or person without taking the time to consider other possibilities, a hungry little Imagiphant grows and grows.

The Imagiphant
(ee·maj´·eh·fent)

These might be the hardest elephants to free because doing so requires us to consider that we could be wrong and may have to view someone we've struggled with in a different light. Our brain wants completion. We have a desire for understanding and certainty even when things are complex, so when we don't have all the data, our mind fills in the gaps. In the absence of information, we create our own stories. As humans, we're far more likely to interpret someone's intentions as unfavorable because anticipating negative situations helps us protect ourselves.

When there's an Imagiphant in the room, it's not just about misjudging someone else's intentions. Sometimes we have to reevaluate our own intentions. This makes the Imagiphant hard to spot on our own. You may need someone else to help you, a copilot, to keep an eye out for Imagiphants in your path.

An Imagiphant Case Study

Awhile back, I was having lunch with a good friend of mine, a colleague who does somewhat similar work in leadership consulting. I had shared with him a new story/concept that I was creating related to leadership work. After our lunch, he followed up with me and asked if he could share my story in his newsletter.

When I got the email request, my amygdala got a little prickly and then protective. My brain was spinning quite loudly on this thought: "But wait! That was my content. I wanted to be the one to share that information."

Because of my work with mindfulness and working with great therapists, I can typically catch and observe strong, unproductive emotions fairly quickly. Typically. I believe in coming from a place of abundance. I also happen to have a great deal of love and respect for this friend. So I was caught off guard with my own threatened response.

I tried to observe the thoughts and to get curious with it but found myself battling with the tension.

My husband Nick happened to walk in the kitchen while I was processing. When he asked what was wrong, I said, "I'm having an interesting moment right now and trying to stay curious." I explained the situation, my resulting reaction, and how I was trying to figure out the best path forward.

Now you have you understand that one of my personal missions I lovingly and playfully describe is to rid the world of shitty managers. As Nick is familiar with this mission, he said, "Yeah, I can understand your frustration. The question that's coming up for me is, do you want to rid the world of shitty managers like you've said, or do you want to be *the one* to rid the world of shitty managers?"

Boom.

Nick's insight was exactly what I needed to reshape my perspective. My imagination was telling me a story that this colleague might negatively impact my work. But the reality is that the content needed to get out, regardless of my attachment. My colleague wasn't co-opting my content; he was helping me with my mission.

Without Nick's input, the story I was telling myself could have impacted my relationship with my colleague and limited the reach of that message, missing the chance to connect with people who needed to hear about the concept through him and not me.

This brings up an interesting sidenote on Imagiphants: once we are able to get space from a situation and test our stories, sometimes we can look back and realize we couldn't remember what upset us in the first place! To this day, I couldn't tell you what the content was that I created that triggered me at the time, but I'll never forget the emotional journey it took me on.

What You Might Hear if an Imagiphant Is in the Room

The language we hear around an Imagiphant signals anti-curiosity and tends to be resigned to the situation. To correctly identify an Imagiphant, listen for phrases like:

- "No, I know that's what they meant."

- "Oh, that's just who they are."

- "I don't need to ask. I just know."

- "They will never be open to that."

Questions to Ask if You or Someone Else May Be Feeding an Imagiphant*

- What do I know to be true?

- What role am I playing in this?

- What assumptions am I holding?

- What makes sense to the other person?

In the case of the Imagiphant, remember, you may need to brainstorm with another person to come up with other possible intentions behind the situation that has troubled you. Healthy flocking in action! It's also important to note that sometimes, your assumptions may be correct.

BLAMING:
OWNING THE BLAMEPHANT

One of the most common ways to feed a Blamephant—another pesky species of Avoidephant—in a team is to blame the leader. In a survey I conducted to study trust in leadership, an overwhelming number of respondents mentioned frustration over leadership inaction as a barrier to trust. Many sentiments revolved around statements like "My leader could see the elephant (the avoidance of the issue) and didn't do anything about it."

At some point, we've all been in a situation where we know there's a barrier, and instead of taking action, we blame other people's inaction for that barrier. When we complain instead of acting on problems, there's a good chance we have a Blamephant in the room.

The Blamephant
(blame´·eh·fent)

There are, of course, situations when the person with formal authority absolutely needs to be the one to take action. However, this does not mean they hold sole responsibility for every team issue. Sometimes we're waiting for our leaders to be superheroes that swoop in and save the day, but we should remember that leadership is not a role; it's an act. It is a skill we can cultivate in ourselves. When we make a leader the scapegoat for team inaction, we not only stunt our own potential, but we also hold back our team from success.

A Blamephant Case Study

In my career, I've seen the following scenario play out many times: a leader of a team has an employee—one who is a high performer in the technical sense, but a poor performer when it comes to interpersonal or collaborative work. In other words, this person has toxic energy and is causing confrontation or creating issues that bring everyone down. A brilliant jerk.

But the leader does not fire that person. Heck, maybe that person even gets promoted because of their technical skill.

All the while, though, the leader *blames* them for the issues. Though the leader has the authority to make a change, they don't hold the employee accountable or take any ownership over the situation.

They may say, "Well, that's just how so-and-so is," instead of coaching or fixing the problem.

We often hear stories of how employees blame their bosses, but the scenario I've described above is important too. Elephants walk both ways.

What You Might Hear if a Blamephant Is in the Room

The language we hear around a Blamephant abdicates our responsibility. If there's a Blamephant in the room, you might hear (or catch yourself saying):

- "Can you believe they did that?"

- "I don't know why they made that decision."

- "It's not what I would do, but…"

- "I really hope (insert manager name here) talks to that person. She never…or He always…"

Questions to Ask if You or Someone Else May Be Feeding a Blamephant*

- What would success look like in this situation?

- What haven't I tried yet?

- What steps could I take to help resolve this situation?

- What do I gain when I feed the Blamephant?

In the case of the Blamephant, remember, it is easier and less risky to blame than it is to own. Owning your role might not require you to speak up, but it will require you to stop speaking around.

NUDGING:
NOTICING THE NUDGEPHANT

A Nudgephant is a medium-sized Avoidephant. It's smaller than an Imagiphant or Blamephant, making it a little harder to spot. We feed a Nudgephant when we see a barrier, and instead of addressing the issue directly, we try to nudge our team forward with indirect effort. We sugarcoat our words or drop hints instead of making statements. When we're dealing with a Nudgephant, it means we've worked up a little bit of courage to approach an issue, but it might not be enough. If you and your team are dancing around an issue without diving in to address it, you may have a Nudgephant in the room.

The Nudgephant
(nuj'·eh·fent)

It's important to note that nudging is not always a destructive behavior. Nudging can also be a safe way for people to engage with a situation. Sometimes, a well-executed nudge allows a team member to spur action without creating resentment or to create an opening to discuss a difficult situation. A nudge can turn the heat on just enough for change. If you nudge and it works, it's fine.

Nudging behaviors only create a Nudgephant when it becomes clear that a nudge is not enough to improve the situation, but we keep doing it anyway. If we don't change tactics at this point, we're inviting a Nudgephant to take up residence in our relationship.

A Nudgephant Case Study

Early on in a meeting with my team, my colleague Kristin brought up a frustration. She said sometimes she feels that we put time into creating tools for collaboration but don't follow through to use them. She was not wrong. I could sense, though, that she was hesitant about sharing this information, and it was clear that she had been struggling with it for a while, unbeknownst to me.

After thanking her for bringing this up and reflecting on what I could do differently, I asked what had held her back from bringing this up before. She replied that she'd mentioned it in passing but felt it was my job to put the tools into action.

"If there are things you see that we're creating but not using, please know that I might not realize it," I said. "As you know, my ADHD can make it hard to follow structure and attention to detail. That isn't an excuse, and I'm actively working on it and always try to be transparent. When you notice it again, would you say something? That would be incredibly helpful."

"I kind of feel like I do speak up," she said. Then, with a smile, she said "Maybe indirectly."

Teresa, another member of the team, jumped in.

"How about we all just say what we need? Let's just get honest."

All of us laughed. As a group, even though we are passionate about the work of uncomfortable conversations, we still have moments where we sidestep issues, and we all appreciated Teresa's willingness to call out the Nudgephant.

What You Might Hear if a Nudgephant Is in the Room

When a Nudgephant is in the room, you'll hear a lot of passive language that is delivered in a roundabout way. To correctly identify a Nudgephant, listen for phrases like:

- "I tried to have the conversation, but..."

- "You might want to consider..."

- "Maybe we could..."

- "Do you think it might make sense to..."

Questions to Ask if You or Someone Else May Be Feeding a Nudgephant*

- What is the impact I want my message to make on the situation?

- How can I confirm that they understand the message I've attempted to convey?

- How else could I say this message so it could be more easily understood?

- What would it look like to be direct and kind?

In the case of the Nudgephant, remember that while the understanding of the message lies with the listener, your delivery will set them up for success.

DEFLECTING:
QUIETING THE DEFLECTEPHANT

It's usually fairly obvious when there's a Deflectephant—one of the largest species of Avoidephants—in the room. I'm certain you've experienced one. When a situation gets uncomfortable, the Deflectephant likes to whisper in the ear of the office jokester or quickly shift topics. A Deflectephant gets a handful of peanuts whenever someone makes a joke or displays sarcastic, self-deprecating behavior or attempts to create a detour in response to an uncomfortable situation.

The Deflectephant
(dah·fleck'·ta·fent)

Allowing a Deflectephant in the room can waste time, hurt psychological safety, and shut down team members.

The Deflectephant aids diversion. When someone is unwilling to be vulnerable, they may attempt to minimize or hide their own discomfort by creating discomfort in other people or creating a distraction.

It can be extremely hard to work with the person creating a Deflectephant. Someone feeding a Deflectephant might want to change the subject or quickly move to resolution without properly exploring the problem. They might have a hard time taking things seriously when a situation gets uncomfortable, possibly resorting to disruption and sarcasm, hiding in the image of being a jokester or "class clown." If another team member raises an issue with this behavior, it's common for the person feeding the Deflectephant to claim that the other person "can't take a joke," even though the manipulative, critical behavior they're exhibiting is not actually humor but passive-aggressive avoidance.

When the Deflectephant turns toxic, the triggered responses go well beyond joking, and veer toward discrediting, manipulative, critical behavior that crosses over into contempt. Deflecting behavior can turn contagious or attract other elephants. If team members feel jokes are made at their expense, they may begin to guard and shut down. If not kept in check, communication can devolve into quips and jabs, making it almost impossible to address serious issues without first freeing the Deflectephant.

A Deflectephant Case Study

Recently, I worked with a team that was struggling with a low level of trust and safety. Team members did not seem encouraged to share ideas or solve problems. Morale was suffering, and their productivity was not what their leader knew it could be.

When I walked into the conference room for my first team meeting, Zach, a senior member of the team, shouted, "Well, let's see what you've got, Sarah!" His behavior raised my elephant radar immediately because our work was focusing on trust, which requires a level of vulnerability. Because I know that people will use humor when uncomfortable, I took an internal note and proceeded with our work.

As the meeting went on, the jabby outbursts from Zach continued. It was apparent that Zach's defense mechanism of choice was making sharp, sarcastic comments that degraded, minimized, or discredited nearly every topic we discussed. We had a giant Deflectephant in the room, sitting right on Zach's lap, and that elephant was hurting the team's ability to achieve a sense of psychological safety.

When team member Kayla began to wade into a tough conversation, sharing her vulnerable perspective, Zach cracked a cutting joke. Kayla shut down, reversing on her brave statements and minimizing the problem she'd tried to address.

"I want to make an observation. I appreciate humor and sarcasm as well as the next person; it's one of my love languages. And I also want to make sure we honor what is being shared." I turned to Kayla. "This is a real concern of yours, right? I want to make sure we're hearing all of this."

Kayla admitted that her issue was of serious concern. Other teammates chimed in to agree and offer solutions. I realize that as an outside party, it was easier for me to create a sense of safety for Kayla by naming the Deflectephant and carving out room for her to speak. It can be extremely hard for someone being targeted by Deflectephant behavior to continue honestly sharing their perspective. If no one had spoken up in support for Kayla or if

Kayla hadn't taken a stand, I believe the conversation would have ended and we would have missed the important perspective she brought to the team.

What You Might Hear if a Deflectephant Is in the Room

The language we hear when a Deflectephant is in the room can act like a joke but has an undercurrent that is cutting and aggressive or dismisses the seriousness of the concern. To correctly identify a Deflectephant, listen for phrases like:

- "I don't think it's that big of an issue."

- "Let's just agree to disagree" (without meaningful conversation).

- "It was a joke. You just can't handle sarcasm."

- "You're too sensitive."

Questions to Ask if You or Someone Else May Be Feeding a Deflectephant*

- What is being avoided in favor of deflecting?

- When are we moving on too quickly without exploring or resolving?

- How might this humor be inhibiting honest conversation?

- Are these jokes targeting a team member's vulnerability or our team's psychological safety?

In the case of the Deflectephant, remember that often the goal is to dismiss or distract. A powerful way to navigate these is to acknowledge or restate the importance of the conversation at hand. Sometimes it takes another person to speak up to reiterate the importance.

WHAT'S NEXT?

Sometimes the process of identifying elephants is uncomfortable, but I want to take a moment right now to reassure you. If you have identified your own behavior in this examination of elephants, it's okay. We cannot free what we cannot see! Identifying elephants is a skill you can develop over time to help you work toward increasing your self-awareness and strengthening important relationships.

Once you've searched your office for signs of the members of the Avoidephant family—the Imagiphant, Blamephant, Nudgephant, and Deflectephant—be on the lookout for elephants that combine traits. Sometimes a Nudgephant has dominant Imagiphant genes. A Nudgephant can also employ deflection. It's not uncommon for one elephant to attract another. For example, if a Blamephant is on a rampage in your office, some team members might start feeding a Nudgephant as an attempt to dodge blame. One thing to remember is that we might all avoid the conflict in different ways in different situations.

Perhaps your office has created a unique variety of elephant. If you feel you have a new species marching around your cubicles, take some time to observe its characteristics and give it a name.

Even though this process can be uncomfortable, it's important work. Once we correctly identify an elephant, we can begin the process of freeing it. Now that we know our elephants' names, in the next chapter, we'll take a look at how you might be encouraging them to stick around by feeding them.

Get Curious

- What elephants are common in your world?

- What have you observed in yourself, others, and teams to help you see an elephant might be getting created?

- What other elephant types have you experienced? (Share your insights with me on social @sarahnollwilson!)

4

Are You Feeding the Elephant?

I don't know what it is about feeding animals, but I find it completely delightful. One of my fond childhood memories is about feeding a wild squirrel when I was ten years old.

First, I started laying down crackers with peanut butter. I just fed it a little bit. Then it began to connect me with food, so it kept coming back to me. I switched to putting a spoon of peanut butter out, and then once the squirrel got used to the spoon, I held the spoon, and the squirrel would come and eat from my hand. At one point, I got the really smart idea (remember, I was ten) to reach over and start petting it, and it let me. Video evidence exists. The longer I fed the squirrel, the tamer it became.

Years later when I was at Universal Studios, I noticed a bunch of people feeding a squirrel. Of course, I wanted in on the situation, and I had sunflower seeds in my backpack (just for such an occasion), so I started feeding the squirrel too. But this squirrel became aggressive. It wanted to crawl into my backpack, and crawl on me, but not in the kind, safe way I had hoped. I thought this squirrel was just a sweet little thing, and feeding it was a benign action, but all the people who fed this squirrel had contributed to its aggression and rewarded its presence. By feeding the squirrel, I put myself in the middle of a situation that was out of hand.

The elephant in the room works the same way. The first time the elephant appears, we don't realize the consequences of feeding it. But the longer you feed the elephant, the easier it gets for the elephant to hang around. It's hard to predict when an elephant might turn aggressive or what kind of destruction it could cause. Our avoidance can sometimes create as much damage as the conflict we are trying to navigate.

Are you giving life to this situation by feeding the elephant and helping it grow? There might be short-term comfort in attributing complete responsibility for an elephant to someone else on your team, but when you deny your involvement, you're contributing to long-term conflict. **If there's an elephant in the room, everyone owns it.** So, if you see an elephant and don't work to acknowledge and address it, congratulations! You've just given it a peanut.

Wait. Did you think you weren't an elephant feeder, and this was just a chapter for other people? Are you feeling a little panic at the idea that you've contributed to the situation at hand?

Darlin', we are all elephant feeders at one time or another. Don't beat yourself up. I'm in it with you, and we're going to arm you with curiosity and the tools you need to free those elephants.

WHY ARE YOU FEEDING THE ELEPHANT?

Why are you feeding an elephant instead of plunging in with a solution or exploring the situation? Why is it so hard to talk deeply with those we care about? All of your intentions for how you want to show up with your team are so beautiful. They're positive and aspirational and inspirational. And yet, sometimes, we just don't come through the way we want to. There are times when we don't show up at our best, or we're misunderstood, or there's a gap in communication, and we start tossing peanuts around.

Before we can stop feeding an elephant, we need to know we're feeding it. This level of awareness requires us to admit that we might not be showing up the way we want to, and that can be hard. It's uncomfortable when we realize our actions don't line up with our vision of ourselves. It can seem easier to leave it all unexamined.

"Without reflection, we go blindly on our way, creating more unin-tended consequences, and failing to achieve anything useful."

—Margaret J. Wheatley

Once we realize we're feeding elephants, we can explore why we prefer tossing peanuts to having an open conversation with ourselves and others or why that might be a safe option. Following are some of the common reasons we resort to feeding elephants; feel free to add your own.

We Want Less Risk, More Safety

In a workshop once, someone asked me, "Why is it easier for me to talk behind someone's back than to address them directly?"

The risk is lower, right? Part of the reason it's easier to talk around someone is that it feels like the risk is lower to the person you're talking about, but, more importantly, the risk is lower to us. When someone says, "Oh, I don't want to hurt someone's feelings," what they're also saying is, "I'm worried what they'll think of me if I do hurt their feelings."

We can hide the fact that we're feeding an elephant by "venting." Typically, when we vent, we are seeking validation for our point of view. Sometimes we do need to process strong emotions and also validate the impact of our situation. If talking to someone else first helps regulate emotions, opens up possibilities, and helps you potentially have the conversation later, great. If talking is just to make you feel right, not always great.

This desire for safety and fear of conflict can come from a variety of places, from cultural background to family upbringing, or a lack of confidence and skills. But there is one more reason that is often whispered during breaks or shared privately during virtual sessions far more frequently than one might suspect. And that is trauma. Whether it was growing up in a family where if you spoke up or out, there were consequences, sometimes dire. Or in relationships where advocating or wanting something different could mean your world and worth was diminished. Or working in an environment where command and control reign supreme and collaboration and creativity are only words on the wall.

As humans, we are constantly calculating the risk of the situation versus the potential gain or benefit, consciously and unconsciously. Will there be retaliation? Will there be damage? Will I be excluded? Our interpretation of the data before us is heavily influenced by our lived experiences.

We're Afraid of Loss

When I facilitate workshops, I'll often ask who agrees with the idea that people fear change. Inevitably, every hand will go up. Then, I'll ask who is like me and doesn't carry a ton of cash with them.

Then, when people raise their hands, I'll pick a random person and hand them twenty dollars, saying, "No strings attached."

The person I give the money to is always a little confused. I assure them they can keep the money, but I need them to answer a few questions.

"Was that scary for you?" I ask.

Usually, they say no.

"But your situation has changed, right? Now you have money, whereas before, you didn't."

They always agree.

"We just said people fear change, right? But this wasn't scary. Why wasn't this scary?"

The answer almost always revolves around the idea that getting the twenty dollars was a positive gain.

From this example, we can see that it's not that people fear change, necessarily. It's natural to evolve. None of us is the same person we were this time last week. Our resistance shows up when we are—or are afraid we are—losing something. **People don't fear change; they fear loss.**

This loss can take many forms in the workplace or in our relationships, such as fear of retaliation or exclusion. Sometimes this can also mean a fear of losing power or authority. None of us *want* to harbor these emotions, and many of us aren't always aware we are.

With this in mind, when we scramble to feed an elephant instead of addressing an issue, it's usually helpful to look at possible points of loss to consider why we might be courting chaos instead of seeking solutions.

We Feel Accomplished or Powerful

Finally, feeding an elephant can make us feel like we're taking action when we're not actually doing anything to resolve the situation. Blaming or criticizing someone behind their back is a way to exert power over the other person or the situation and stoke our false sense of control.

Even complaining, in a way, is a version of us feeding elephants because the shadow intention of pointing out what is "wrong" about someone else allows us not to point that finger inward and see ourselves.

We can also feed an elephant to preserve power or authority. Truthfully, I have seen this more times than some people may be comfortable hearing. For example, you are a leader and are made aware of inappropriate behavior by someone on your team who happens to also be technically brilliant. You avoid addressing or acknowledging the situation so you don't need to take action. Maybe you wait and hope it blows over or minimize the situation's real impact. The team members negatively impacted by this person's behavior end up leaving, or worse yet, harmed, because it becomes too much. You continue to feed the elephant instead of freeing it. That is until the situation starts to negatively impact you. Say your leadership or board starts to question why you have high turnover and wonders if you are the right person for the job. Now suddenly, the peanuts stop and you start taking action but often not ownership.

If the situation above sounds specific, it's because it is, and it's a fairly common scenario I've observed. We may continue to avoid addressing or acknowledging a harmful barrier so long as it isn't harmful to us. In effect, the elephant is created to protect ourselves regardless of the damage it is causing to others. What makes this scenario so tricky is that our self-protection is so strong and automatic that we may not even realize we are doing it. But we are, and we can work to do better.

HOW ARE YOU FEEDING THE ELEPHANT?

Some of the ways we feed elephants are so deeply embedded in our habits and in our culture that we don't see the behaviors for what they are. Here are some ways we might be feeding an elephant without even knowing we've been leaving a trail of peanut shells in our wake.

We Avoid Asking for What We Need

Sometimes we confuse discomfort for being direct. It's very easy to feed a Nudgephant, for example, without realizing it. Put simply, if there's something you need from somebody that they don't know you need, or you don't communicate, it can cause a barrier. When you don't let that person know what you need, the elephant will grow and grow. The challenge is that sometimes we don't realize the reason we are frustrated with a person or the situation is because we have a need that's not being met.

Once, in response to the question *How have you fed an elephant?* a survey respondent wrote: "Somebody tried to call the elephant out, and I got mad at them." I appreciated their honesty and would have loved the opportunity to dig deeper with them. What was it that triggered their anger? Anger is considered a secondary emotion, meaning it is fueled by other emotions. It shows up when we are trying to protect from other emotions, like fear, humiliation, sadness, shame, and hurt. As you can imagine, it can feel even more vulnerable to admit you feel hurt or shame, and so anger rises to defend.

When anger and frustration show up, these are cues that we have needs that are unfulfilled. They may be needs of being heard, being included, being respected, or being safe. When working with people navigating frustration and anger, it's more common to focus our energy outward, towards or at someone—i.e., blaming—rather than focus that energy inward to examine those potentially unmet needs.

> *Blaming is a way to protect your heart, trying to protect what is soft and open and tender in yourself.*
>
> **—Pema Chödrön**

We generally don't like to admit this, but I'm going to put it out there anyway: feeding a Blamephant can provide us with a zippy little endorphin boost. In addition, blaming a situation on someone else allows us the illusion that we're absolved of responsibility—and again, allows us to avoid asking for what we really needed in the first place. Blamephants are especially tricky because they appear to feed us too.

We Talk to the Wrong Person

Instead of bringing up an issue to the person involved, we talk about it with another. As we discussed in Chapter 2, "flocking" is a common stress response and also an effective way to feed the elephant when the goal of the conversation isn't clarity or closure.

Again, sometimes we do need to talk to someone else to process strong emotions, consider perspectives, and explore possibilities of how to move forward. Later in the book, we will talk about the importance of having someone be your copilot and serve as a loving critic. The challenge is that when we seek out people who will only agree and validate, we may have found a partner to feed that elephant with us instead of freeing it. The people who validate may also allow us to ruminate instead of processing.

There are times when having someone validate our experience with "Yeah, that was inappropriate what he said" is important. That validation can give us clarity, which can give us courage. Courage to answer these questions, what do we do with this information? What conversation do I need to have with myself? With that person? Or potentially with another party that could impact the situation (i.e., HR)?

We Hold Untested Assumptions

Sometimes we take the information in front of us and create assumptions that become the regulating rules by which we make sense of the world. This could be assumptions based on past experiences, information we've gathered, or connections we are

making. **When other people don't behave in a way that makes
sense to us, it's because they're busy behaving in the ways
that make sense to them.**

> *"Reality doesn't just happen to us. We are continuously construct-
> ing it."*
>
> —Robert Kegan and Lisa Lahey

Adam Grant explores this idea in his book *Think Again: The Power
of Knowing What You Don't Know*. He explains, "We're swift to
recognize when other people need to think again...Unfortunately,
when it comes to our own knowledge and opinions, we often favor
feeling right over being right." Sometimes we create elephants
because of past experiences. Just because that assumption was
true before doesn't mean it will be true now.

Testing assumptions can feel risky because it requires us to test
beliefs we have about ourselves and the world, and it is possible
we will discover something new and different. Testing assumptions can also feel risky because doing so could validate the very
reason we are avoiding the situation to begin with.

We Defer to Someone Else

It's incredibly easy to feed an elephant in the name of "not wanting to step on anyone's toes." We can slant this to pretend we're
being respectful. Or we can villainize the leader for not seeing or
acting on a problem.

If you have the authority to address a problem but defer to leadership, or HR, or a coworker, you're wriggling out of doing the hard work that comes with being a responsible team member. Not only that, but you're feeding an elephant. If you don't have the authority, though, getting the information into the right hands is an important role.

Some of the Ways I've Fed an Elephant

Here are ways I've caught myself feeding elephants. We all do some of these at one time or another. Fess up. Which ones feel familiar to you?

- Saying "it's fine" when it isn't (It's never fine when we have to say it is, right?)

- Having a meeting after the meeting

- Refusing to talk about it

- Minimizing it

- Convincing yourself that "this too shall pass"

- Hoping someone else will say something

- Changing the subject

- Filling an uncomfortable silence

- Making light of the situation

- Thinking, "it's not my problem"

- Getting defensive

- Gossiping

- Blaming

- Triangulating (playing people off each other to get a desired result)

- Sugarcoating

- Rushing an uncomfortable conversation

- Moving too quickly to resolution instead of taking the time to make sure you understand

- Deferring to leadership/HR

- Not taking ownership for a role

- Filling in a lack of data with doubt and suspicion

- Discrediting attempts to address the elephant

- Dancing around the elephant, complaining

- Addressing a group when the issue is with a specific person

- Being more interested in what's most comfortable instead of what's best for the team

- Settling instead of advocating

SHAME, SHAME, BOOMERANG

Now that you are paying attention to ways you might be feeding elephants, you might not always feel great when you catch those moment. Remember, any time we work on identifying thoughts or behaviors that are different from how we want to show up, it's hard work. It's easy to fall into a shame spiral and self-flagellate. *Oh, man. Here I go, feeding the elephant again!* Or *Yup, I'm avoiding. Like I always do.*

I see the following cycle constantly with my coaching clients (and let's be clear; I've also done it myself).

When a client plans to focus on identifying the elephants they're feeding and the behaviors that are getting in the way, I warn them about the impending shame spiral. But sometimes, people will fall into what I call a shame, shame, boomerang. They correctly catch the shame spiral they're about to slip into, but then they shame themselves for shaming in the first place. The shame bounces between those two tight walls (like a game of Ping-Pong or Pong), and it's a painful cycle to break.

The mantra I hold on to in response is simple and powerful: **Celebrate the catch.**

If we catch ourselves behaving in a way that is different from how we want to show up, it's a moment to be celebrated because that's the moment you get to make a choice. Sometimes, catching that moment of choice is even harder than shifting gears to do the right thing. And we can't change course if we don't know what road we are on.

Every time you catch yourself saying, "I'm not good enough," or whatever words are your personal shame refrain, I want you to say, "Oh, I caught it!" Then pat yourself on the back. By calling it out, you're building a muscle of awareness that sets you up to catch these moments sooner in the future.

When we're working on recognizing our behaviors, we aren't striving for perfection; we are looking for progress. Perfection is not realistic. I don't expect anyone to catch themselves before they feed an elephant the first time out of the gate. You might look back a week later and say, "Oh, I was totally feeding the elephant in that situation."

The more you practice, the more quickly you'll be able to make the catch, which is of great impact. As you speed up your recognition abilities, you'll shorten the window of time available to employ destructive behavior as a reaction to uncomfortable feelings. You'll cease to sacrifice time and energy to the distraction of the elephant. Eventually, you'll be able to catch yourself as you're pulling a peanut out of your pocket, and you'll get to make a conscious decision about feeding the elephant.

Sometimes, when you make the catch, it might be easy to laugh about your elephant feeding on your shadow intentions. Sometimes, the elephant you've fed has created a serious situation, and there's no humor to be found. Even when the catch means you'll have to face significant challenges or make substantial repairs, at least take a moment to celebrate that you caught yourself.

How I Learned to Celebrate the Catch

After my panic disorder diagnosis, I would say things like, "I wish I didn't have to deal with this. I wish I could go back to normal. I wish things were how they used to be." Those thoughts caused me a great deal of suffering. Going back to the way things had been wasn't an option. But every time I had that thought, it set off a spiral of tears and awful feelings that could last for days.

Learning to catch myself as I thought or voiced those regrets was an essential part of my recovery as encouraged by my therapist. Sometimes, I needed my husband Nick or my therapist to catch it for me because I couldn't see it in the moment, but the more we all pointed it out, the easier it was for me to recognize the behavior.

At first, I'd catch the fact that I was feeling down, and I could trace my steps backward and understand why. Then instead of taking a day or two to realize what had happened, I started noticing that I felt down fifteen minutes after saying those words. Eventually, I could catch the words coming out of my mouth. Then I got quick enough to catch myself before I said anything that made me feel worse.

WHAT'S NEXT?

Much of the time, when you're feeding an elephant, it's because your brain wants to protect you, so it crafts scenarios or nudges you toward defensive behaviors. And sometimes we need those protections. The challenge is knowing when to have the courage to step from behind the protection and pursue the possible partnership or pursue advocating in ways you haven't before but need to now.

*But Sarah...*I imagine you thinking...*Sure, I didn't address the elephant. Maybe I talked to Shanice when I had an issue with Charlie. But have you seen Bob over there with his bucket of peanuts? He's dumping them in piles all over the office, attracting Imagiphants and Avoidephants like it's feeding time at the zoo. You haven't said anything about all those other people who feed elephants.*

I know. I'm sure it hardly seems fair that we've focused on all the reasons you've been feeding elephants, but here's the thing: all the reasons you have for feeding an elephant are the same reasons other people are feeding the elephant too.

It's so simple, but so easy to forget. Everyone feeding an elephant is trying to manage fear and discomfort, feel a little more powerful, chase an endorphin hit, or save someone's feelings. They're employing the same behaviors for similar reasons. And since we are the only ones we can control, we have to start there.

You aren't alone in any of this, so when we do the work of freeing an elephant for ourselves, we can bring empathy into the conversation with others. I feed elephants. You feed elephants. Together, if we talk about the elephants, we can find a way to stop feeding them. In the next chapter, we'll explore how to do just that.

Get Curious

- Think of a time when you struggled with a change. Looking back, what did you lose, or what were you afraid of losing?

- What ways have you fed an elephant?

- When did you hold an assumption that turned out to be different than what you initially thought?

Part 2

THREE STEPS TO FREEING THE ELEPHANT

5

Step One: Be Curious with Yourself

Now that you've come to terms with the existence of the elephant, you've classified him, and you know you're at least partly responsible for keeping him around, it's time to stop feeding him. The best way to do that is to talk about the elephant.

But wait—does that idea itself send shocks through your nervous system? Isn't it interesting how our gut reaction to the idea of discussing an elephant is to turn around and immediately feed an Avoidephant?

I know it feels uncomfortable and possibly scary to think about having a conversation about an elephant, whether with yourself or someone else. Here's the good news: sometimes just noticing an elephant *is* enough. But in many cases, if you don't talk about the elephant, it keeps getting fed, and it sticks around.

At the end of the day, though, that elephant doesn't want to be in the room. Even more importantly, you don't want it there. Here, we'll discuss practical ways to set your elephant free. A hint? The core of this work is a Curiosity-First Approach.

THE APPROACH

One thing to remember as we venture into strategies is that there isn't a script or a formula where you will instantly and effortlessly free elephants. Often, people will ask me to simply tell them what to say. While I will share tips and tools, every situation is different, and this work requires you to dance in the moment. Doing this work requires equal parts curiosity and courage, but don't worry; we will help you develop your muscles for both!

What I have found in my decade-plus of research, observation, and experimentation is that while situations are always different, there are core practices that will increase a successful freeing of an elephant.

The Curiosity-First Approach to freeing elephants follows three specific practices:

- Be curious with yourself.

- Be curious about the other person.

- Be curious *with* the other person.

We will examine tips and techniques in each of these core practices to help you free the elephants in your world—and we'll start right where it begins: with the self.

WHY CURIOSITY?

Humans, by nature, are all capable of profound curiosity. We're wired for it. It's how we've evolved and why we're different from other species. I especially love this quote from John Lloyd. "Pure curiosity is unique to human beings. When animals shuffle around in the bushes, it's because they're looking for one of three things: food, shelter, or sex. And it's only people, as far as we know, who look up at the stars, and wonder what they are."

The truth is that while we're born curious, as we grow older, we can shut down our curiosity in a variety of ways. The good news? This is reversible, and for some it never went away.

THE CURIOSITY ZONE

I once came across a definition of curiosity in a dictionary as "Seeking to learn the unknown." What I'd like to add is "and knowing there's always an unknown." In *Curious: The Desire to Know and Why Your Future Depends on It*, Ian Leslie wrote, "Curiosity starts with the itch to explore." To be curious requires intellectual humility. It requires us to own and explore that we don't know. Tenelle Porter, a postdoctoral scholar in psychology at the University of California, Davis, describes intellectual humility as the ability to acknowledge that what we know is sharply limited.

Great leaders don't just value curiosity; they role-model and they advocate for it in everything they do.

Great leaders aren't curious only when it serves them or when it is easy.

Great leaders aren't conditionally curious; they are chronically curious.

Being chronically curious means to explore and respond to possibility.

Being chronically curious is a gift to ourselves and those around us.

What do I mean, exactly? When we are doing the work to free elephants, we are really building and rebuilding relationships. When we are building and rebuilding (and sometimes healing) relationships, it requires us to look deeper at ourselves and beyond ourselves. Curiosity is a powerful vehicle to get there.

The Knowledge Sweet Spot

Daniel Berlyne is a psychological researcher who is fascinated with why people get interested in some things and not others. One of his experiments involved talking with people about many types of birds and then asking follow-up questions to assess their curiosity level. They found that when people already had some awareness about a particular type of bird, they displayed greater curiosity in the conversation. When they'd never heard of that bird, their curiosity waned significantly. Curiosity also declined when a subject had a high level of knowledge about one specific bird mentioned to them.

What does this mean? When we don't know anything about a subject, we don't tend to exhibit curiosity. When we know too much, we start to lose curiosity. The prime zone of curiosity falls in the space between knowing nothing and thinking we know it all.

Think of curiosity as a bell curve. On one side is the climb to gaining enough knowledge to get curious, and over the top of the curve is the decline where we begin to overestimate how much we know.

This curiosity curve is apparent when observing relationships. Often the elephant is created because there is an increase in the assumptions people bring to the table when they know too much or too little about a relationship, the situation, and the other person. When people exist at either end of the curve, they don't stop to ask curious questions about themselves, the situation, or the other person's experience.

You Can't Be Too Curious

While I was working with a team on navigating elephants, a woman raised her hand.

"But can't you be too curious sometimes?" she asked.

Obviously, I was curious about what inspired her to ask this as I sensed she was thinking of a specific situation. I had a feeling there was a specific scenario behind her question, so I asked her about it.

"Well, when I do something my husband doesn't agree with, he'll barrage me with questions like "Why did you do that?" or "Why did you think that was a good idea?"

"Oh, okay," I responded, taking a deep breath. "Knowing what you know about curiosity, how would you define those questions?"

"I don't think they are questions at all! He disagreed and couldn't say it," she laughed.

She was right. Sometimes people will hide judgments, frustrations, or accusations behind a question mark. It is essential to understand that the intention behind a question is what matters. A question like "What were you thinking?" is not a question of expansion, so it shuts down possibility and exploration. When you ask accusatory statements hidden in questions, you're rolling a barrel of peanuts into the room, or worse yet, you are putting up a barrier where the elephant might never be freed. You're not actually addressing an issue, and the people around you are going to frantically throw food to their elephant of choice.

> ## *It's Not a Curious Question If...*
>
> - you already know the answer;
>
> - you already have a position and are guiding the person to your position;
>
> - you are pretending not to know;
>
> - you don't want to know the answer; or
>
> - you are looking for validation or reassurance of your idea.

IT STARTS WITH YOU—AND WHY

The first step we always need to take when we start to see a possible elephant is to start with ourselves. If I become aware that I or other people are avoiding talking about something that is impacting our success, before I jump into that conversation, I need to get curious with myself. Getting curious with ourselves helps us understand what is important to us, what we need in a situation, the role we played, and most importantly, what our perspective is on the situation. This information not only brings clarity to us but also improves the likelihood that we can bring clarity to the conversation if one is needed. It can also help us step into our courage when needed. If we fail to take this step, we may run into not communicating our needs, we might miss opportunities to see other perspectives and take ownership, and we may limit possibilities to move forward.

Where do you begin, then? If you are observing an elephant, that tells me you are likely connected to the situation, the team, or the relationship being impacted—and it's time to go to work. Here are three powerful benefits of seeing and owning our role:

- When we can acknowledge and own our part of creating the elephant, even if it is tiny, and share that with the other person or team, we create an invitation for them to see and own their part. We can also learn from that moment and apply that insight to future situations.

- When we can clearly see what is important to us, we can communicate with greater nuance and potentially be open to what is important to the other person.

- When we can first give ourselves grace for the role we've played, it can be easier to give someone else grace for their role.

How might this look in a real scenario? Let's look together.

HOW TO GET CURIOUS WITH YOURSELF: A CASE STUDY

Laurel, a member of a team I coached, received an email from her boss, Judy. It said only, "Hey, can you send the file on the Johnson account?"

"Wow, that was rude," Laurel said, showing me the email.

"Well, how do you know there were rude intentions behind it?" I asked.

She shrugged. "I just know."

Here's a hint: If you catch yourself saying the words "I just know," often that means you have shut down your curiosity because you believe you've already got it figured out. Laurel was feeding an Imagiphant.

Together, Laurel and I started working through a series of questions I use to identify and test assumptions. We were able to come up with plenty of possibilities to account for the brief and direct nature of the message. Is it likely, based on previous experience, that the manager was being rude? Yes. Is it possible she wasn't? Also yes. The truth lies somewhere in between.

Here are the questions and Laurel's answers to give you a guideline for how to approach each one.

Q: What Do I Know to Be True? (Observable Facts)

A: "What I know to be true is that Judy sent me an email and didn't say thank you. That's all I actually know. I don't know why she worded the email the way she did. I don't know what her situation was. I may be pulling from previous experiences and assuming I know more than I do."

Q: What Do I Need to Confirm?

A: "I need to confirm what Judy's intentions were. I took her email as rudeness and assumed Judy was angry with me, but maybe the situation was urgent, or she was trying to type out an email while talking on the phone."

Q: Is My Reaction about Preference, Process, or Performance?

A: "Judy didn't actually do anything wrong. She needed information, and she asked for it. She wasn't mean or disrespectful, just direct. I think because I always make an effort to soften my requests with pleasantries, I expect other people to do the same and feel slighted when that doesn't happen."

The Result

Considering possibilities beyond rudeness helped Laurel open up to the idea of discussing the situation when she ran into Judy in the break room later.

"Hey, that email felt a little terse," Laurel said. "Is everything okay?"

"Oh, I'm sorry," Judy said in a clearly apologetic tone. "I was working through so many emails. I know you need Accounting to approve funds on the Johnson project, and I couldn't find the information I needed to push it through. I didn't want you to have to wait on me anymore."

When Laurel reported back to me, she said, "As we talked further, I realized that Judy always means thank you, because she's thankful for me. She also values efficiency, and she's showing her appreciation by not wasting my time."

Judy's email wasn't a performance issue, but it felt like it because Laurel's personal preferences were creating a barrier. Once they talked about the email, they were able to find common ground easily. If she received a similar email in the future, Laurel could say, "Oh, I know that Judy values efficiency, and if she had an issue, she would tell me. Once Judy learned about Laurel's communication preferences, she began making an effort to add a note of acknowledgment to future emails.

If Laurel had fed the Avoidephant instead of examining the situation around Judy's email, she would have held the assumption that Judy was purposely harsh (a performance issue), and their relationship could have rapidly devolved. By tapping into the mystery and asking curious questions, Laurel used the opportunity of a misunderstanding to strengthen her relationship with her boss.

YOUR SELF-CURIOSITY QUESTION TOOL-KIT

The work of getting curious with ourselves requires us to conduct "fearless audits" to ask questions that help us uncover what is beyond the surface, to seek out the unknown, even if it is uncomfortable. Exploring ourselves through the lens of a fearless audit needs a healthy dose of courage as well because we might discover something new about ourselves, we might discover something difficult, or we might need to face something we've known but have managed to avoid.

There is not a limited, single set of questions for us to ask because every situation is different. However, I will share with you the top questions I've gathered, created, and tested in my work that can be applied to many situations. You don't need to ask yourself all of these questions, but choosing some will create a powerful place for you to start.

What is my perspective on the situation?

Taking a moment to simply capture your perspective is powerful. Notice I'm not asking you to state what the situation is, but rather your perspective. Our words matter, and the word perspective is intentional. As much as we can feel like our experience is the truth of the experience, every person involved will see it differently. Before we can move forward with any type of conversation, we need to make sure we can clearly see and state our experience.

The easiest way is to finish this statement: "My perspective of that situation is..."

For example, you may say, "My perspective is that at the last team meeting, we kept talking about solutions and didn't take time to fully understand the problem."

What do I know to be true?

This is where we start to dig into our perspective and challenge ourselves to examine it more objectively. Our brains are so good at making interpretations about why something happened the way it did or why someone behaved a certain way that we need to create space between what we observed and our interpretation.

Another way to approach this question would be to say, "If someone were watching what happened on video, what would they see, hear, or notice?" Again, our goal is to look at the observable behaviors. What is said/unsaid? What is done/not done? For example, if I said, "Wow, James was rude because he didn't say thank you when I stepped in to help." That might be true, and there could be other interpretations. What do I know to be true? James didn't say thank you and I know how it made me feel.

What do I need to confirm?

Once we have identified our perspective and clarified what we observed, it can be helpful in some situations to understand what we might be missing. This is where we need to test our assumptions about the situation or the person or gather additional missing information. When we look at assumptions, it isn't that they are untrue, but they are unexamined. Often situations involving humans are complex, and our assumptions work to simplify. Those simplified ideas/assumptions can get in the way of understanding a complex situation.

According to Robert Kegan and Lisa Lahey, who tackle the idea of assumptions powerfully in their seminal work *Immunity to Change*, "Big assumptions are like a good lawyer when they are true, but when they aren't true, it is like an embezzler stealing options." And the goal of identifying what we need to confirm isn't about blowing up the assumption, but learning about it. To be clear, through this entire exploration of the Curiosity-First

Approach, you may end up validating or confirming your initial assumption is correct, and you may discover something new. Both outcomes are powerful because they come from choice instead of chance.

Is this a preference, process, or performance issue?

If you created or fed an elephant in response to someone else's behavior, it is critical to ask this question. In his work on marriages, Dr. John Gottman observed that sixty-nine percent of all issues in relationships are perpetual, meaning that it is a difference in style or needs. One of the biggest traps I see people fall into—especially leaders—is confusing the preference or process with a performance issue. We all have preferred ways of how we like to communicate, approach our work, navigate our relationships, eat our food, etc. Because our preferences feel right to us, we think they should be right for everyone else. What can happen is that we think because it's different, it's wrong.

My colleague Gilmara Vila Nova-Mitchell, a DEI Leadership Consultant, recently shared a powerful insight about someone in her life that she often thought of and described as "being difficult." Words I have definitely thought and said. She shared, "You know, Sarah? I realized it isn't that this person is difficult. That's a label, and our words matter. It is just that they are difficult for me, and our styles are different." Considering the situation through a new lens opened up a new possibility to think, feel, and do differently.

Ask yourself honestly: Is this a difference of preference? Is there an issue with the process? Or is this truly a performance issue?

What role did I or do I play?

In my experience, exploring and owning your role is the hardest of all the questions to explore. This question challenges us to consider that not only may we have contributed to the situation, but maybe we didn't show up at our best. We are humans with complex egos and images of who we hope to be, and it's not always easy when the mirror shows a different reflection.

Once I worked with a team member who struggled to build trust with her peers. She especially reacted when they would bring corrections to her. I asked her what she did when this happened, and she responded candidly, "I just put my walls up."

I responded, "What happens when you do that?"

"Well," she said, "I make sure they know I'm not listening."

"How's that working out for you?" I inquired.

With a smile, she responded, "Not well."

As she was more willing to reflect on her role, she was able to focus on changing how she showed up.

What bias might I be holding on to?

As we explored earlier, we all have various biases we hold in situations, whether we are aware of it or not. Part of our fearless audit is to take inventory of existing biases we might hold about a person, a department, and a situation. This work challenges us to realize that even in the act of seeking biases and understanding them, we will never see them all. In the world of research, one of the practices is to name and become familiar with biases that may impact the project. The same may be of value when thinking about your relationships. What beliefs might we be holding on to that may impact how we perceive this situation or how we move forward?

Similar to the previous question, this one requires us to look honestly at ourselves without shame or blame to seek a deeper understanding of what is shaping our lens of the situation. For example, as more people worked remotely, there were some who argued or questioned if people could possibly be as productive at home as they were in the office. These beliefs continued even though overwhelming research showed that people were as productive and sometimes more engaged when working remotely.

How do I feel?

Emotions are in us all the time, and we don't often stop to notice, name, and get curious about them. Taking the time to answer the simple question "How do I feel?" can open up insight into what is really going on or help us better understand why we are having the reaction we are to this situation.

> *"Difficult conversations do not just involve feelings, they are at their very core about feelings."*
>
> **–Douglas Stone, Sheila Heen, and Bruce Patton in**
> *Difficult Conversations: How to Discuss What Matters Most.*

Work to be specific with your language. "I feel exhausted." "I feel hurt that I am not being heard." "I feel frustrated and embarrassed." "I feel ambivalent." Remember, emotions are not singularly experienced; it's likely you are experiencing many emotions when you slow down enough to notice. When we can be present with what we are experiencing, then we can get curious about what might be triggering those responses.

What value of mine is being stepped on or not honored?

Think about a time when you had a strong reaction to a situation. Don't just think of who frustrated you; reflect on what frustrated you. Often when we have a strong negative reaction to a situation (whether we realize it or not), we have a value that is not being met. When you find yourself frustrated with someone or a situation, a great question to ask yourself is, "What value of mine isn't being honored or is being stepped on?"

For example, let's say your leader decides to move forward on a decision without consulting the rest of the team. Multiple people are frustrated but no one speaks up, and as you get curious with yourself, you are frustrated too. Instead of just being frustrated, you get curious about what value is being stepped on. You realize that the approach the leader took feels unfair, and you place a high value on fairness.

What do I need from this situation?

Exploring what we need in this situation serves two purposes. The first is to understand what we need in the situation that we might

not be receiving. Like values, we also have needs. When we struggle with someone or a situation we might have a need that isn't
being met. We all have needs, whether we are conscious of them
or not or express them or not. Maybe you need communication
up front or you need more time to think. The other reason for
exploring what you need is to clarify what steps to take in order
to find resolution...which we will explore further in the next
chapter.

When we don't get clear about what we need in a situation, we
can end up blaming the other person or projecting our frustration onto them, when really, this might not be about a failure on
their part but a missed opportunity to ask for and advocate for
our needs. Looking back at the situation from earlier with my
colleague James not thanking me, what I ultimately needed in
that situation was to be heard and respected.

What would success look like in this moment?

Regardless of what other questions you explore, this is a nonnegotiable point of reflection. When we are looking to understand a
situation so we can resolve it, we have to understand what success
or resolution might look like. When we are in a situation where
stress is escalated, it can be difficult to move from problem to
possibility. Asking ourselves this question moves us from frustration to future possibilities.

I was frustrated with a leader I was working with and Amanda
Trosten Bloom, a leadership and culture consultant working with
us, asked me, "What would you like him to do differently? What
would make this situation better?" Her question caused me to

pause. The truth was I hadn't even considered those questions. Sometimes when our brain is so full of stress, it can't see solutions.

WHAT'S NEXT?

For many who live in NYC, there is a deep love of the city, a connection to it that you don't often see elsewhere. When the pandemic devastatingly hit NYC, I received a message on Twitter from my fellow HR pro and dear friend Laura Mazzullo, owner of East Side Staffing, based in Manhattan. She had made the difficult decision to stay with her parents in Connecticut until things settled down.

She sent me this message:

> *I know you like a little light bulb moment...I thought of two words that have been triggering shame and tension for me: "STILL" and "YET."*

> *So, I looked up the definitions for both and they imply inaction (eek!)*

> *"Back in the city YET?" "Still with your mom and dad?" "Any business yet?"*

When people would ask her questions like these, it caused a reaction both about herself and towards the other person. But rather than feel bad or frustrated, resulting in the creation of an elephant, she got curious. Specifically, she got curious about what was really happening in those moments that resulted in her reaction. What I love about this scenario is how she not only got curious with herself, but she got curious about the words to seek deeper insight.

Realizing that words like "STILL" and "YET" imply inaction explained why she felt shame when people asked, as if it implied she hadn't done enough yet or moved fast enough. That language also challenged a few values I know Laura holds dear. For example, her value of action. So when she would hear the words "still" or "yet," it felt like she wasn't doing enough or like the person perceived that she wasn't doing enough, even though she knew she was trying hard to do a lot, given the circumstances. By taking the time to catch the reaction and then get deeply curious, Laura not only got ahead of an elephant, but she got to know herself even more in the process.

When we are curious about ourselves, it not only helps us show up powerfully in the situation, but it also helps us show up powerfully for ourselves. When we have clarity about what is important to us, we can more powerfully speak and stand with courage. And we can do the same for others—which starts, as you probably guessed, with getting curious.

Get Curious

- What makes it difficult for you to get curious about the role you played in a situation?

- Thinking about relationships in your world, what is a nonnegotiable need or value for you?

- What is or has been possible when you've gotten clear about what is important to you?

6

Step Two: Be Curious about Others

Getting curious about ourselves helps us understand what makes sense to us, but since elephants emerge when there are other people involved, it can be equally valuable to explore what makes sense to them.

> "Make sure that you are seeing each person on your team with fresh eyes every day. People evolve, and so your relationships must evolve with them. Care personally; don't put people in boxes and leave them there."

> **—Kim Scott,** *Radical Candor: Be a Kick-Ass Boss*
> *Without Losing Your Humanity*

One way to think about relationships is that we each have our own island where things make sense, where our values rule, and where preferences prevail. I have my island, and you have your island. The goal for building powerful partnerships isn't about one of us packing up and moving to the other side. It isn't about a tug-of-war between the two islands. Instead, it's about coming together to create our island, a shared land that honors us both.

This is hard work. People won't always tell us what is on their island, and sometimes they haven't even named it for themselves. If people don't share what's on their island—don't share their preferences—we can't successfully create a shared space. It makes sense, right? Their island is theirs for a reason. Taking time to get curious about the other person helps us see their island so we can possibly move forward to creating ours together. Full transparency: I learned the hard way how much you might miss when you are only focused on your island and don't explore theirs.

Early in my career, I was working on a major culture project that we'd been asked to move pretty quickly on—too quickly, in retrospect—by our CEO. That meant we sometimes made decisions that didn't follow proper procedure, like having Marketing review all internal communications. It also meant that there were times when the project team missed things, like using the correct font or considering a photo look and feel.

My colleague who was responsible for branding would stop over and point out the mistakes. There was something about how these conversations transpired that never felt good to me. I appreciate knowing what I can do better or what I have done correctly, and what I realized (getting curious with myself) is that I never felt like this was a conversation about how or why we made the decisions we did, just that we were wrong (my perspective through my brain).

I didn't like how I felt after every interaction and found myself starting to avoid her (remember, recovering avoider here), and I knew that wouldn't serve either of us.

I decided I wanted to get real with her and have the important but difficult conversation we needed to have. It took me time to build up the courage, with lots of coaching, but I did it: I pulled her aside one day. The conversation went something like this:

"Hey, can we talk? I don't know about you, but I haven't liked the way we've been working together. I've found myself avoiding you, and I don't want that."

I'd gone into the conversation prepared to be heard and advocate for myself, as speaking directly wasn't always easy for me, which is what I did. Every time she would start to talk about *her* feelings, I'd stop her. Because even though my intention was to resolve the issue, I can see now that my shadow intention was to be heard, not to hear. Until she said something that stuck with me.

"Well, this hasn't exactly been easy for me either, Sarah," she said.

I'd never considered that. So I listened.

"This is such a big project, and I feel like I should have been asked to be involved. It's hard for me to watch from a distance."

It was like the world changed colors. To be clear, there were things I missed and did incorrectly. I'd actually never considered that the root issue *wasn't about me. She was feeling hurt, and I just happened to be a reminder of her hurt.*

Two perspectives, both important. There we were, standing on the skywalk with people passing us by, crying from the emotional release. "How do we move forward in a way that we can both feel good about?" She shared her needs; I shared mine. We committed to honoring both. Not only did our work improve, but our relationship deepened because we knew we could be honest with each other and still be safe.

This was a lynchpin moment for me that showed me what was possible when we were willing (even if not voluntarily, at first) to "rumble with vulnerability" as Brené Brown describes it. Before we step into the arena with someone else, there is an invitation for us to get curious about them.

HOW TO GET CURIOUS ABOUT OTHERS: A CASE STUDY

Years ago, my coworker Paulo confessed to me that his cubicle neighbor Michael was driving him crazy. When Paulo held conversations with another team member, Michael would interrupt the conversation by shouting over the cubicle walls. It was extremely triggering for Paulo, but he didn't know how to talk with Michael about it calmly. So he threw some peanuts to the Avoidephant hanging out in their cubicle block. His ever-increasing resentment toward Michael made it hard for Paulo to ask for Michael's input on shared projects.

"His interruptions are so irritating, Sarah," he said. "I can't take it anymore. What do I do?"

We explored how when we're triggered that way, it's often because our values are being stepped on and/or we have a need that isn't being met.

"When he's doing that, what value of yours is being stepped on?"
I asked.

"Respect and professionalism," Paulo said, almost instantly. The
reason was so close to the surface when he looked for it. "Michael
wasn't invited to the conversation; he's just interrupting."

"Good! That's good clarity, right? Now we can have a conversation about respect and professionalism, instead of just accusing
Michael of being annoying. But I'm also curious; what value do
you think Michael is honoring in that moment when he's interrupting you?"

Paulo's eyes lit up instantly. "Oh shit. He thinks he's being helpful.
Because I know how important it is for him to be helpful. Wow."

With that understanding, Paulo was able to easily figure out the
conversation he needed to have with Michael.

"I'm just going to say, 'Hey, I know you want to be helpful, and I
appreciate that about you, but we have to talk about how you
can do it in a way that feels respectful when I'm having a private
conversation with someone."

Examples of getting curious about someone can look a little lighter
too. Let me share one that made me smile and illustrates how we
can free an elephant without a conversation.

I had just wrapped up a workshop on elephants for hospital leaders, and Romy, the trainer we had partnered with, ran up to me
after our session.

"Sarah!" she said, "I've been feeding the elephant all day."

"What do you mean?" I asked, delighted to hear her adopt this language.

"Well, my boss didn't come to the training, so I asked my coworker, 'Why isn't Donna here?' He didn't know. Next thing I know, I'm asking another person, and another, and not getting any kind of answer. But I kept asking people! I finally realized that every time I did that, I wasn't sending an email to my boss to get a direct answer, and I thought, "I'm literally just flipping peanuts." At some point, it was like, "Here. Here's the whole bushel.""

I laughed.

"Holy shit," she said, laughing with me. "I've been feeding this damn elephant all day while we're sitting in a session on elephants."

YOUR "CURIOSITY ABOUT OTHERS" QUESTION TOOL-KIT

Just as getting curious about ourselves requires us to conduct fearless audits to see what might be hard to see, it can be powerful to do the same for those involved. If our goal when getting curious about ourselves is to understand what makes sense to us, our goal when getting curious about the other person is to become open to understanding what makes sense to the other person.

Again, there is not a limited, single set of questions for us to consider because every situation is different. Below, though, are some powerful questions for you to explore. This portion of the work is about opening your mind to the fact that they have perspectives and values, being careful not to perpetuate your own assumptions. Again, our goal is not to gather the full picture or make assumptions—you won't be able to without having a conversation with them—but pondering these or other questions will help you consider new possibilities and prime you to be more open to perspectives or information you didn't see.

What might make sense to the other person?

No matter how much we might disagree with someone, working to understand their perspective will set up a greater likelihood of resolving outstanding issues. Too often, we can fall into judgment or exasperation when disagreeing with another person. "I just don't understand why he would think that would work!" or "How could she think that was okay?" When I hear statements like these, even when I am the one saying them, it tells me that we have not gotten curious enough about the other person. Seeking to understand and not judge does not mean we need to agree.

What value of theirs might they be honoring? What value is being stepped on?

You've practiced on yourself. Now shift the focus to the other person/people. Based on what you know about them, what value of theirs are they honoring in how they show up? What value of theirs might they feel is being stepped on?

What information might they be missing?

This one is certainly more situational, but sometimes we may have insights or information that the other people do not. Assuming everyone is working from the same playbook can create unnecessary frustrations and is important to clarify if we decide to have a conversation. This is also a good time to go back to ourselves and consider what information we might be missing.

What else might be going on in their world?

What else might be happening in their world that we are aware of? As we've discussed, this doesn't excuse harmful behavior but can sometimes give us insight into what else is at play. As much as we would all love to leave everything at the door, we are humans who are complex, and sometimes that can impact how we show up. As we'll discuss later, intentions don't absolve you from negative impact, but seeing what might have caused the gap can be powerful.

What might they need from this situation?

Just as when we explored this for ourselves, spending time considering what they might need in this situation, either personally or professionally, can help us better understand what makes sense to them and be ready to hear their needs.

WHAT GETTING CURIOUS ABOUT OTHERS IS AND ISN'T

"But Sarah, don't we risk making assumptions or stories when we get curious about other people?" A fair question asked during a recent workshop. The answer is yes, that is a risk. Let's talk about some "watch-outs" to keep in mind when we explore this practice of getting curious about other people:

- Getting curious about others is an invitation, not a prescription.

- Getting curious about others is about being open to possible perspectives you haven't considered.

- Getting curious about others is about opening ourselves up to changing our minds.

- Getting curious about others can open the door for collaboration and cocreation.

- Getting curious about others isn't to fill in their stories, but it is to consider that they have a story.

- Getting curious about others isn't to amplify their needs and dismiss our own.

- Getting curious about others should never be weaponized or used as a way to excuse harmful or toxic behavior.

Sometimes just the act of considering their perspective can be enough to free an elephant, and we may not even need a conversation. Other times, we may leave with more questions than when we started. A conversation or choice happens when our curiosity hits a wall.

WHAT'S NEXT?

Getting curious about other people can be hard. When we begin to pause and allow space to consider the other person, we are able to see beyond the hurt and see the human.

Sometimes an elephant can be freed through the groundwork of these two practices of curiosity. If it can't, the insight you gain in trying can lead to more meaningful communication down the line. Only when we can see our perspective and that of others can we start to come together instead of being on separate islands.

In the next chapter, we will discuss ways to approach conversations to explore differences.

Get Curious

- What gets in your way when you try to get curious about the other person?

- Think about a time when another person changed your perspective. What was the situation and ultimate outcome?

- What traps do you need to be aware of for yourself in thinking about getting curious about the other person?

7

Step Three: Be Curious *with* Others

Once you've taken time to get curious *with* yourself and curious *about* the other person—and if you find that to properly free the elephant (overcome the avoidance and seek resolution) requires a conversation—then it's time for the next step: get curious *with* the other person. This is where you bring your insights to the table to explore.

Take a breath and consider where you've come in your journey.

This is the moment that we might give ourselves every reason in the book to avoid.

You might be feeling scared, uncomfortable, uncertain—name your emotion. And I get it! I got more hours in training to learn to navigate the wheel of a car than I ever got in navigating how to have uncomfortable conversations with other humans. Most of us are showing up from a place rooted in what we learned as children. (I wasn't the first avoider in my family, let me tell you.)

If you are having the conversation, that tells you that this is important and that the potential rewards are worth the potential risk.

But remember this: even if you don't get the result you're after from the conversation, freeing an elephant—which, remember, is the avoidance and not the conflict—can still be worth it. Being present with the hard stuff, and asking someone else to as well, can turn up our emotional heat. We can't always remove the heat fully, but we can do our part to turn it down so we are no longer getting burned.

HOW TO BE CURIOUS WITH OTHERS: A CASE STUDY

Recently, I was called in to work with a team of senior executives. They knew how to have tough conversations about the work, but they couldn't have tough conversations about their relationships. One of the practices we did was an exercise inspired by Kim Scott's work on building cultures, based on her book *Radical Candor*.

Members of the team paired up for a one-on-one conversation that started with "You're at your best when..." Then they'd highlight something they admire about their coworker. After that, they'd say, "Something you might not be aware of is this..." and discuss a habit or behavior that their coworker didn't see. Sharing this unseen behavior wasn't intended to be an opportunity to harm but to—as Dr. Tasha Eurich describes—serve as "a loving critic." Any insights they shared had to come from a caring, respective place. We often think about this like riding shotgun in a car and keeping an eye out for road hazards for the driver or being a copilot.

After they offered these observations to each other, they worked together to answer the question "What can we do to make this a more powerful partnership?"

As I explained the exercise, some of the senior executives were sweating it, shooting me panicked looks. They went into the activity expecting it to be horrible. But after the first round, they all said it was one of the best conversations they'd ever had. Not only were they surprised, but they were proud of each other and felt more connected. They rotated partners, and we kept going until everyone had a chance to pair off. The last conversation was more comfortable than the first, and they went in without dread.

Through the task, they practiced conducting conversations they had been avoiding, which also gave them a concrete example of how to support each other more substantially. Part of what made it powerful is they all committed to showing up with curiosity, candor, and compassion.

DON'T START A STAMPEDE

One of the limiting fears around talking about an elephant in the room with others is the idea that we'll make a bigger mess if we bring up the subject. Truth be told, that could happen if we don't prepare ahead of time to communicate clearly, and sometimes even if we do. The scenario I described above worked because of the commitment by all parties, but I understand this won't be the case in most situations. To be frank, most of the conversations we start won't have all parties committed to showing up with curiosity, candor, and compassion. What then?

Here are some common traps to avoid when approaching an elephant.

Preparing for conflict instead of conversation and exploration

Think about a time when you needed to have a tough but important conversation. Was your heart racing? Did you go through all the what-ifs and worst-case scenarios? Have you ever felt silly when a conversation you'd dreaded wasn't nearly as bad as you expected it to be?

I know when I'm preparing for a tough conversation, my brain starts to slip into defensive mode. I can feel it happening. The idea of potential conflict can trigger our brain to imagine all the possible ways the other parties in the conversation could negatively respond.

Our brain is wired to scan the environment for threats. That's how it keeps us alive as we discussed in Chapter 2. We tend to approach sensitive moments as if we're preparing for battle because anticipating conflict sets us up for survival. But bracing for conflict can cause us to avoid a tough conversation altogether. Or, if we go into that conversation already on the defensive, we risk triggering the other person's defense responses and escalating our own, potentially creating conflict where we could've created cooperation instead.

You might not be able to stop the stress responses, but you can work to slow them down by noticing, acknowledging, and being present with them. My heart races when I speak and stand with courage. Instead of fighting it, I work to feel it.

Working to feel it can be a challenge. First, I check in with myself physically, acknowledging my physical sensations and accepting them as messages that my amygdala is triggered. When I notice this and name it, I'm reminded that I cannot control my biology. Though this isn't overly comfortable, it does make these feelings easier. At the end of the day, being more accepting than adversarial with myself helps me in these situations.

If you aren't in a place to continue your curiosity about yourself, the other person, and the situation, then you shouldn't have a conversation.

When we start from a place of win/lose, we've already lost.

Oversimplifying

We are prone to looking for *a* solution when there may be many. In the search for that single perfect fix, we may oversimplify the situation, failing to realize the dynamics we're dealing with are complicated.

Oversimplifying leads to Band-Aid solutions. For example, if engagement scores are low, a company might decide to give everyone free lunches. Free lunches could cause a temporary morale boost, but it's a Band-Aid that ignores the intricate root system of the problem. Unless the root issue was lunch to begin with, the free lunches won't solve it.

In his book *Curious: The Desire to Know and Why Your Future Depends On It*, Ian Leslie discusses how we tend to approach relationship and communication challenges as if we can solve them like a crossword puzzle that has only one set of words to fit the boxes. He advocates that viewing these challenges as a mystery is more productive because when we approach a mystery, we immediately accept that there are complexities and possibilities to be explored.

I worked with a team that was struggling with trust issues. Terry, the senior leader, was technically smart, and knowledgeable about the business, but often verbally abusive. A brilliant jerk. Terry's behavior created an environment that wasn't psychologically safe for his team or anyone who worked with him. Turnover and complaints to HR continued to increase. As an attempt to solve the problem, the company sent Terry to a class on effective communication. This course of action is common in corporate environments. When there's access to training, sometimes training becomes the hammer that makes everything look like a nail. However, a three-hour communication workshop was unlikely to change Terry's behavior and the issues of distrust it created.

That's not to say that a three-hour workshop on communication isn't ever helpful. After exploring underlying issues and motivations, a workshop could be an effective way to introduce skill-building of critical communication and trust concepts and deepen self-reflection, but sending someone to a lunch-and-learn isn't a fix-all for complicated issues.

In this situation, for example, it could be easy to oversimplify and say the issue was with Terry. But what was also true is that he worked at this company for decades and was promoted. Action was not taken until formal complaints were made. What was it about the culture that tolerated this behavior? What changed to cause leadership to take action? What competing commitments were at play that not only approved of this behavior but rewarded it? What did we need to create to ensure this behavior wouldn't emerge again?

Only looking at the elephant through our own lens

We all show up in the world in ways that make sense to us. If you have a conflict but haven't asked yourself the question "What makes sense to the other person?" you're falling into this trap. Often, we only look at the elephant through our own lens, without considering the other person's point of view—because doing so means we have to give ourselves space to be wrong. (Let's give ourselves permission. Say it with me: we are allowed to be wrong!)

As we explored in the previous chapter, we get so focused on our perspective and our needs that we don't often take the time to consider what the situation actually means for the other person, or what's been going on in their world. When we only look through our own lens, we limit what might be possible.

> *"The big shift here is from wanting to 'be right' to wanting to 'get it right.'"*
>
> **—Brené Brown**

Holding the belief that if you bring up a problem, you have to be the one to solve it

One reason people have shared that they hold back on addressing an elephant is that while they can see the issue, they aren't sure what to do about it. We've all heard the maxim "If you bring me problems, you better bring me solutions." I've worked for many people who have said this and have repeated it myself. What I have come to see is that sometimes what we have to offer our team is a clear-eyed view of the problem, and providing our perspective is what opens the conversation for someone else to bring a solution to the table.

Bringing up a problem doesn't give you ownership over the solution. It's unlikely that one person owns the entirety of the problem and could therefore bring a whole, workable solution independently. This traditional belief of only bringing problems that you have solutions for is limiting at best and could be devastating at worst.

When we recognize that there's an elephant, our first job is to simply shine a light in that direction so you and your team can start exploring together. The truth is, if we are dealing with an elephant, there likely isn't a quick fix. If there were, we might not be in this situation. Some situations can be solved with quick fixes with our current authority and expertise. But so often, elephants emerge from the system. When the problem lies in the system, then it requires the system to be part of the solution.

The desire to seek certainty and simplicity is strong in our work cultures. When we are met with complex situations, people aren't prepared for how to navigate. Consider the COVID pandemic: everything was disrupted, and there was often no clear or obvious path forward. The leaders who sought out certainty consistently struggled with the chaos. When we are dealing with humans, there will always be uncertainty.

Change the maxim for yourself: regardless of who brings up the problem, we all need to be open to exploring, experimenting, and evolving to move forward.

YOUR "CURIOSITY *WITH* OTHERS" QUESTION TOOL-KIT

As much as I wish I could give you a script that would remove all of the discomfort, ensure understanding, and create collaboration, I can't. No one can. The more important the relationship or the situation, the bigger the risk. The bigger the risk, the higher the emotional heat. Uncomfortable or emotionally charged conversations simply can't be scripted. They aren't a play, but an improvisation that requires us to both be and dance in the moment. However, like for any good improvisation artist, there are tools we can lean on and use in the moment. There isn't a formula, but there is a flow.

1. Prepare for the Conversation

To prepare for the conversation is not about what you are going to say, but to define what the goal of this conversation is. What is the impact you want to make—on the other person, on yourself, on the situation, on the relationship? Examining these questions is critical, and also helpful, because it can help turn the heat down a bit at the start. You cannot control other people, but what you do control is your role in the conversation. When you are clear about the impact you hope to make, reflect on the following: Who do you need to be and what do you need to do to show up intentionally? Do you need to be present, firm, curious, open? Do you need to ask more questions and interrupt less?

Taking time to prepare for the conversation can create an anchor for you that will help you not to just have good intentions but to take intentional action. When we are clear about our intentions, sharing them with someone can be a powerful place to start a conversation.

- "I haven't been clear with you about how I am feeling, and I owe it to you to be more honest."

- "I want to talk about our project. I'm struggling with direction and want to explore with you."

- "I want to talk about when you made that comment yesterday. I don't think this was your intention, but the impact was that the team felt dejected."

2. Share Your Perspective by Inviting Their Perspective

As we've explored in many stories, we can be so focused on the role someone else played that we overlook the role we played. When you invite another's perspective from a place of genuine curiosity—remember, not a place of "winning" or "convincing"—you open the door to real communication. There is a place for telling or selling, but relationships are built in the land of discovery.

Consider using the specific language of perspective. It signals that you know there are multiple viewpoints and that you value understanding theirs. "I'd like to talk about that meeting. I want to know your perspective and to share mine."

Speak in questions, not absolutes. Instead of saying, "This is what happened," say, "This is what happened from my view, and here's how it made me feel. Can you tell me what you see and how *you* feel? I'm listening."

3. Create Clarity, Changes, and Closure

Conversations will result in a combination of increased clarity, changes made, and/or closure. Sometimes you may experience all, and other times you might only get one. For example, when you reach clarity, maybe you now know what the other(s) involved will or will not do. Maybe you've gained a better understanding of what's important to you or your ideal route forward. Or maybe the clarity has led to more and better questions that are yet to be explored. Perhaps, too, change is in the cards—for you, for the relationship, or for the future. For example, maybe your manager takes your feedback and makes changes to policies, or maybe you and a colleague commit to changes to be more honest with each other. Either of these can lead to closure if you choose for it to—and you get to decide what that looks like. It might not be the closure you want, but you can reach it.

When you are in disagreement with someone, a way to move forward could be to say, "Knowing what we know now, where do we go from here?" Then, look for a way to compromise and create together moving forward.

That, however, is the best-case scenario. Sometimes, having clarity can give you a different kind of closure and inspire a different kind of change—one where you may need to accept something may not turn out like you planned, or where the person is unwilling to listen, change, or collaborate. In Chapter 11, we'll discuss what happens when the other person isn't ready to move forward with you and how to navigate these situations. However it ends up, I hope you're a little lighter for having freed the elephant.

Bonus: Take It to the Team

The above flow is person-to-person, but a bonus to this process is that it applies on a larger scale too. The context may change based on how many people are in the room, but that's an issue of scale, not practice. You still follow the flow: prepare, share your perspective and invite theirs, and create from differences. You're just doing more of it, and likely in a bigger room (as opposed to sobbing one-on-one on the skywalk while people walk to lunch—which, as we know, I have also done).

WHAT'S NEXT?

Effectively approaching an elephant isn't always easy. To have conversations that truly matter, we have to choose to be curious about ourselves and our relationships, despite our discomfort.

It's easy to be curious when a situation is benign and there's a high level of psychological safety. It's much harder when the stakes are high and you start feeling threatened and want to armor up. Remember that your thoughts and feelings may work in resistance to the way you want to show up in a conversation. That's okay. Even though I do this work with regularity and help others have these conversations, I still have times when my nervous energy or those protective feelings well up. "I don't want to be curious!" I'll think. "I want to tell that guy he's wrong!" or "I feel sick just thinking about this conversation." Observe the way you're feeling, honor it, and focus your *actions* on the impact you want to have. When I feel myself becoming guarded or prone to judgment, I think, "Be curious, be curious, be curious," as a mantra to keep me on track, then I take a deep breath (or a sip of water) and ask a curious question.

Curiosity is entering a different door to get to the same room and likely leaving a different way than you came in. When you choose to take the curious door, you'll find a path toward the meaningful conversations you need to have.

Our goal is not always to remove discomfort but to minimize damage. Our goal is to hear and be heard. If you want to get better at having at these conversations, you need to do the work, over and over and over again. People evolve, relationships evolve, and situations evolve. Even when these connections are good, these conversations can still feel hard. Practice may not make it easy, but it will make easi*er*.

In our next chapter, we'll cover some common reactions and sample conversations you may encounter as you free the elephants around you.

Get Curious

- What language or phrases would you use to invite a conversation, explore possibilities, and/or advocate? The language I stated feels right and true for me, but it might not fit you (or the situation).

- When was a time you were worried about a conversation, and it turned out better than you thought? What was the situation? What contributed to the shift?

- When was a time you approached a conversation that didn't turn out how you'd hoped? How did you feel? What became clearer for you as a result?

8

ALL Together: Freeing the Elephant

In a recent coaching session, one of my clients was discussing an elephant situation using The Curiosity-First Approach. He believed his staff felt comfortable coming to him with hard feedback. In his mind, he could not fathom why someone may feel timid in the safe space he thought he had created. When I encouraged him to get curious about how others may feel when he encouraged them to offer feedback on his management style—specifically, a colleague with whom he'd had an especially challenging relation-ship—he turned to me and said something I'll never forget:

"I would have never considered his perspective if you didn't ask me to."

That response signifies the beauty—and the challenge—of this work. It requires us to look outside ourselves—and *inside* ourselves—at how we perceive others and how we are perceived *by others*. It all comes down to getting curious, candid, compas-sionate, and courageous.

That said, the steps to bringing it all together to free the elephant need not be laborious or a feel like a huge, insurmountable process. At its core, it goes something like this: "Hey, what's really going on with me? What might be going on with the other person? What impact do I want to have right now? How can I use what I know about myself and this person—and what I'm curious about—to have a meaningful conversation?"

Let's look at this process a little more in depth.

MINDSETS FOR
MEANINGFUL CONVERSATION

When we're preparing for an important conversation or we know that we're going to have a conversation that's uncomfort-able, there are a few core mindsets that we have found in our research that are more likely to set it up for a successful expe-rience.

Again, there is no script. I am reminding you of this for a reason: it may sound cliché, but you're dealing with other humans who are bringing their *own* experiences and their *own* amygdalae to the table. They're not only having this conversation—they're also receiving it. And ultimately, the goal is to have the best outcome for all people involved, right? And to do that, you need to be intentional.

I'd go so far as to say that if you have not done this prep work, wait until you have before having the conversation if that is an option. Otherwise, you may run the risk of showing up unregulated, incurious, or insincere, and your chances for success decrease drastically.

Words create worlds

If your team knows the language of elephants, it can be helpful to use the language and shared understanding to say, "I want to make an observation. Is that an Avoidephant? Can we talk about it?" If elephants are not part of your shared language yet, you can approach with something simple, like "This is how I'm feeling," or "Hey, I'm noticing this," or "This is my perspective. What do you think? Anyone else feel this way?" Through this questioning, you'll be able to identify allies who have also felt the presence of the elephant and can help you continue the conversation.

Keep in mind, we know that everyone takes a different amount of time in processing. If, for example, you and your colleague were both aware of an elephant, and one of you wanted to say something like this at your next meeting, it would help to share with the other person in advance. Then they could have time to think about their respect and be ready to reply in a meaningful way to move the situation forward as an ally. Otherwise, unintended friction might arise if you felt like you were left hanging, alone without backup.

Get on the balcony

Sometimes it helps to take a different view of the situation. As Ronald Heifetz and Marty Linsky share in their work on Adaptive Leadership, we spend most of our time on the dance floor. We see what is in front of us and around us but not much beyond. Getting on the balcony invites you to imagine yourself observing from a distance, as if you're in the balcony of a theater, watching the show. Now you can see the system and patterns you couldn't see on the dance floor. This view is especially helpful in seeing the patterns that surround a situation, and it's often in the patterns that possible insights and solutions lie. Practices for you to consider:

1. Designate someone from the team to be "on the balcony" during meetings and share observations and connections to previous meetings. For example, "X is coming up again and it sounds familiar to Y from our last two meetings."

2. At different moments, invite the team to "get on the balcony" and ask what they see in themselves and the group as a whole.

3. At each moment, practice stepping "on the balcony" to observe the energy of the room, the nature of the discussion, and the dynamic between people. Make note or share out loud. "I'm on the balcony right now and I'm observing. What do other people notice?"

Don't attack...invite

Focus your intentions on inviting others to have this conversation with you, especially when working in a group. Notice who is participating and also who might need a more specific invitation to share their perspective. In coaching, we have the philosophy that your intuition is always right, but your interpretation of your intuition might not be. Even though you may approach the conversation with clarity about your thoughts and emotions, there will likely be things you don't know. When you are having a conversation with others look for opportunities to uncover that information together so you can all gain greater clarity.

Also, be sure to only speak to your experience. If you know your colleague Farah has had a bad experience with X, don't share Farah's story. If she's quiet, you could invite her to add something, but let people own and tell their own stories.

Here are some examples of how to invite others into the conversation:

"I'm noticing we haven't heard from the rest of the group, and I'm wondering what we are missing."

"Anyone else notice the room just got really heavy? Or is it just me?"

"I'm on the balcony and want to make an observation…"

Hold still in the silence

There may be uncomfortable silences in conversations about conflict or differences. By not rushing in to fill the silence, we allow everyone space to synthesize their thoughts. Make sure you're allowing yourself that space too. My favorite practical tip is to always bring a glass of water with me when working with a team. Taking a sip when I need to pause and think keeps me from feeling self-conscious about that extra moment, and prevents others from attributing meaning to the silence. When an elephant is getting freed and silence emerges for a length of time, especially in a team setting, a powerful question is "What is the silence telling us?"

Seek self-awareness

Stepping into conversations related to elephants is always an act of courage—but for a different reason than you may think. Yes, these are opportunities for us to explore and find resolutions to difficult situations, but they're also opportunities for us to learn *about ourselves*. If we're only coming from the perspective of "how do I change the other person?" then we will miss a beautiful opportunity to transform ourselves. As my colleague Dr. Teresa Peterson often shares, "We don't grow by being around a bunch of people like us. We grow through challenges, new perspectives, and new ways of doing."

Listen to learn

We know that as humans, we are more likely to build trust when we feel heard. While most of us would like to think we are exceptional listeners, the reality is that there are a lot of factors working against us, making it difficult for us to listen completely and deeply. At any given moment, we're taking in something like eleven million pieces of information. Can you believe that? That means listening to learn is a conscious act that takes effort. We are seeking to learn about the other person, about ourselves, and about the situation so we can create the best possible outcome *together*. A simple practice is to notice when you are listening from a place of responding or waiting your turn. If so, really challenge yourself to listen to learn something new about yourself, about the other person, or about the situation.

Honor human complexity

This mindset might be one of the most important ones in this work—which is why we dedicated a whole chapter to the brain! Humans are amazing, complex, and messy. That can be exhausting, frustrating, and overwhelming...especially when we're trying to build relationships. Understanding and honoring human complexity is so important because it helps us give grace and space—to others and to ourselves. When we can give grace and space to ourselves as we're processing these emotions, it becomes easier to extend the same to others.

Speak and stand with courage

To speak and stand with courage requires us to step outside our comfort zone—which, as we learned in our discussion of psychology, is not intuitive. At its very core, the act of freeing the elephant is an act of courage. Speaking with courage is not just acting from a place of assertiveness or advocacy; it is also being willing to ask questions, exploring the unknown, and showing others compassion and empathy *even when you may disagree*. The act of standing with courage is to be able to hold steady in the heat. Which may look like staying present and not retreating, advocating and not avoiding, speaking firmly or perhaps a little softly. Speaking and standing with courage means we walk into the fire and know we will walk out. I've never met an elephant that didn't raise the heat in me, in the room, or in other people. Our ability to face that heat curiously, compassionately, and courageously is the crux of this work.

THE MOST COMMON REACTIONS
WHEN FREEING ELEPHANTS—AND
HOW TO NAVIGATE THEM

Before we dive in, take care to remember two important factors when navigating these conversations: first, our interpretation of things may not always be accurate. Said another way, although our intuition as humans is fairly accurate, our interpretation of a situation may not be.

Second, we should remain adaptable, even though we have more conversation tools. Why is it important to be adaptable? Because often in these emotionally charged moments, we're dancing with partners we have never rehearsed with. Though it's helpful to know some basic steps, we need to be able and willing to dance in the moment.

Keep these concepts in mind as you explore the following common responses to freeing elephants.

Common Reactions and Sample Responses

Viktor E. Frankl said, "Between stimulus and response there is a space. In that space is our power to choose our response. In our response lies our growth and our freedom." I agree.

What comes before our ability to internalize that wisdom, though, is a conversation about the difference between a reaction and a response. When we react, we're on autopilot. We just *do*; we don't *think*. When we respond, as Frankl says, we add a little space in there. We let some air into a situation. We are intentional and thoughtful. We would all rather respond than react, right? But of course, we are all human—so we're going to cover both.

The following is not a comprehensive list of every reaction you may face or response you might consider. Why? Simple: that list doesn't exist. But it *is* a distillation of common scenarios, and it will be helpful as you approach what a particular uncomfortable conversation might look like for you.

As you navigate these emotions, remember that the strategies I'm offering are possibilities. I'm offering the language I would use, but play with it. Make it your own. I invite you to try these phrases on and create from them in a way that feels authentic to you.

Also, keep in mind that repeatability in this process is important. If you begin having uncomfortable conversations today, you might not even realize you're building that muscle for something you need to be ready for in the future.

These conversations won't always end gracefully. The reality is that part of being human is facing conflict, challenges, and difficult situations. And being part of great teams means we will and should disagree. But the more practice we have—such as moments of preventing an elephant or recovering quickly when we slip up in confronting one—the more we can help strengthen our relationships, not only with the people around us, but also with ourselves.

BEING DEFENSIVE

As we learned in Chapter 2, when we feel threatened, it's natural for our brain to go into protection mode. This isn't always a conscious choice; more so, it's how we're hardwired.

That said, there's a coaching technique called powerful observations, from the work of Co-Active Coaching, that can be incredibly effective in situations where you perceive someone is shutting down in defensiveness, denial, or another related emotion. Basically, you share what you are observing and ask them their thoughts. It's pretty simple in theory but can be hard in the moment: have them validate if your observations are accurate. You might be surprised. (Tip: even if you're accurate in the first place, giving them the chance to pause and reflect may allow them space to shift into a more productive emotion.)

Here's how this may look:

"I noticed you got very quiet when I gave you that feedback. What's going on?"

"I'm sensing that you put up a wall after that last comment. How true is that?"

These approaches won't take away the defensiveness, necessarily, but they can test your assumptions. For example, one time, a manager tried this, and her team member responded that they were feeling more embarrassed than defensive. Needless to say, that changed the whole tone of the interaction and led to an entirely different conversation.

> **Try this mantra here:** "Exploration over exasperation."

BEING ANGRY

A response born of anger can look many different ways. It could present as aggression, passive aggression, the need to assert or reassert dominance, the propensity to make personal attacks or raise their voice, and so on. All of these responses are unproductive. (In fact, I'd venture so far as to say that **the most effective way to develop an ineffective relationship is passive aggression**, in particular.)

A technique you can use here comes from behavior coaching amplified through Brené Brown's work: "honor the emotion; coach the behavior." All emotions are okay, but all behavior isn't.

Read that again if you have to. It's a good one!

Emotions are not good or bad, inherently. They just *are*. It's what we do with the emotions that can become unproductive.

Here's how this may look:

You bring up a conversation with someone. Before you can finish, they raise their voice and start speaking aggressively over you. You could instead say firmly, "It's okay that you're angry right now, but it's not okay that you're talking over me."

Do you see how powerful that is?

By taking this route, you're not diminishing or discounting how the other person is feeling. Instead, you're acknowledging that their experience and feelings are valid, but it's their behavior that's ineffective, and you're setting a boundary.

Note: Of course, your safety is priority at all times. If you ever feel like you're in an unsafe or retaliatory environment, throw "working it out" out the window and do what you need to be safe.

Try this mantra here: "Their reaction is about them, not about me."

BEING DISMISSIVE

A dismissive response from someone can look a number of ways.

"Don't worry about it."

"I don't see what the big deal is."

I think we've all likely heard this a time or two.

Sometimes, dismissiveness comes from a place of good intentions. Sometimes, the other person truly does not want us to worry and is not placating. And sometimes it comes from a place of dismissing what is important to another person.

To move toward freeing an elephant in this dynamic, try the following:

- Say, "What I need right now is for you to hear what I have to say and not dismiss it."

- Say, "I don't think you are hearing how important this is to me."

Here's how this may look: Maybe you're struggling with something that made you uncomfortable at work, and you bring it up to a coworker. You may say, "Hey, can we talk about how that meeting went down today?" In that conversation, she may mention that she didn't think the off-color comment that was made was a big deal, or that it was just a joke. "This may not be a big deal to you," you can reply. "But it was a big deal to me."

When approaching these conversations, work to stay regulated when possible. Note that being regulated doesn't mean stoic, dispassionate, or without advocacy. Rather, it means being able to navigate extreme emotional escalations that derail you, impact them, and shift the conversation. Biologically, we know that if two people are emotionally dysregulated, it is a greater likelihood that they will escalate each other instead of de-escalating. That said, every situation is different and requires different energy. Sometimes increasing our emotional energy can create a necessary sense of urgency. Turning up the heat can transform as much as turning it down can.

> **Try this mantra here:** "Regulate the heat."

BEING UNCOMFORTABLE OR AWKWARD

If you haven't committed this to memory by now, it's time: dancing in the discomfort is the name of the game. It's good to be uncomfortable, as that's when we grow. It's also hard to be uncomfortable, as we're all human.

It's also important to recognize that awkwardness is a pretty normal reaction when you begin to show up differently in conversations. It makes sense, right? If you've always been a yeller versus a talker or a teller versus an asker, your colleagues might be skeptical of you at first because they're not used to communicating with you in these more thoughtful ways.

Here's how this may look:

- Extended silence

- Shifting physically, fidgeting, heart racing

- Lack of eye contact

- Half-jokes about "trying out your training?"

To move toward freeing an elephant in this situation if you're the one struggling with awkwardness, try the following:

- Say, "This isn't easy for me to share and might not be easy for you to hear, but it's important."

- Say, "I'm not going to get this right the first time, but I want to try."

- Say, "I can sense that this isn't easy to hear, but I appreciate you listening to it."

When we are feeling awkward or uncomfortable, our stress responses can kick in, moving us to take action to change the situation without resolution. We cannot always go around discomfort; sometimes we have to go through it for the greatest impact. In these moments, think about anchoring yourself so that you can hold steady where you are, in this moment, in this discomfort.

Try this mantra here: "Hold Steady."

BEING RELIEVED AND APPRECIATIVE

In many cases, the reaction you are faced with when you have an elephant-freeing conversation may be the opposite of the one you were worrying about.

You may hear something like "I'm really glad you brought this up," or "I feel so much better." These engagements bring us closer together and help us reconnect.

Here's how this has looked for me: I had a colleague, Katie, who was instrumental in helping me create efficiency and structure in my business. As we grew and evolved as an entity and a team, it became obvious the need for her role as it stood was no longer there. I knew I had to tell her, but I didn't know how she would take it. Would she feel left behind? Upset? I focused on the impact I wanted to make, to share my appreciation and define the path forward. I really cherished our relationship and wanted to ensure that what on the outside could have seemed like a transactional conversation didn't *feel* transactional. First, I owned that I hadn't done the best job of keeping her in the loop as things had changed—which was part of the root of my discomfort. As a result of my unintentional approach, our relationship had lost clarity.

It turned out Katie not only felt the same, but she could also tell it was weighing on me and suggested ways for us to work together in a different capacity more suited to both our needs moving forward. I was relieved, and she appreciated talking through things.

When the conversation ends up where you were hoping or even better, take time to acknowledge that. Not only is this an opportunity for you to show appreciation to your partner, but it's also an opportunity to reinforce the habit for both of you.

You might consider the following:

- Say, "I'm really glad that you brought this up and we could talk about it."

- Say, "I'm so glad we can talk about the hard stuff."

- Say, "Grateful that we can have these conversations."

> **Try this mantra here:** "Acknowledge, appreciate, repeat."

WHAT'S NEXT?

In Part 3, we'll move from theory, strategies, and practices to what you need to internalize about yourself as an elephant freer and receiver. Keep this in mind as we march onward: the basis for many of the best practices we've covered so far, by the way, is not only what we all have in common but also how we differ.

For context, remember that when attempting to create an environment where it's possible to have vulnerable conversations and talk about freeing the elephant, it's important to remember that not everyone is going to have the same ability to see elephants, nor will everyone on your team have the same level of comfort addressing elephants.

How can you show up thoughtfully when the other person doesn't? How can you approach these tough learning opportunities ahead?

Let's get started and find out.

Get Curious

- There are times when we need to advocate and hold steady for what we need. What was a time when you advocated for yourself or set a boundary? What did you learn from the experience?

- What is a mantra you want to hold on to for yourself to anchor how you want to show up in a conversation?

- Conversations that are emotionally charged can be draining, mentally and physically. What are some things you can do to ensure you recharge after a conversation?

Part 3

STOMPING ONWARD

9

Receiving the Elephant: The Self-Awareness You Didn't Know You Needed*

*Or thought you already had!

"I don't understand why people don't feel they can talk to me when they're having challenges," Bob, the CFO of a company, said to me. *"I have an open-door policy."*

I could appreciate Bob's struggle, as the feedback I was sharing wasn't easy for him to hear. In fact, the receiver of the message is just as—if not more—important than the person delivering the message. Because they ultimately decide what information is understood and acted upon.

I knew Juliana, who worked under Bob and managed a team of twelve, had told me in confidence that she never felt like she could disagree with him because he became aggressive and defensive. I was seeing that in action as we were discussing a topic separate from her challenges.

"Why are they coming to talk to you, Sarah?"

Bob then turned his focus to Juliana.

"I mean, you trust me, right? You can talk to me. I'm approachable?"

Of course, Juliana said, "Yeah."

I didn't jump in because it wasn't my place to approach something Juliana told me in private. There was a reason she didn't feel safe in that moment, and I knew we would have a follow-up conversation later. I reflected: How many times had I held back information from someone, and they walked away thinking they had proven they were a safe, trustworthy person? And how many times did I make it unsafe for someone to share? The elephant was raising its trunk and trumpeting, but Bob and Juliana couldn't hear it.

OUR SELF-ASSESSMENTS ARE FLAWED

Fabio Sala, a leadership researcher, published his study in 2003 exploring the discrepancies between self-assessment compared to other people's experiences. He assessed over twelve hundred people in various leadership positions. He had participants assess themselves, had others evaluate them, and then studied the gaps in perception and reality. He found that when compared with individuals holding lower-level positions, higher-level employees consistently showed a more significant discrepancy between how they viewed themselves and how others rated them. This is partially explained by the idea that the more experience we have, the more likely we are to overestimate our competence. It's also a direct effect of power dynamics. People are less likely to give feedback to those in positions of power. Makes sense, right? If you control my wages and opportunities, I'm much more likely to be more cautious in giving you feedback.

Positions of power can paralyze perspectives. The word "power" is uncomfortable for some people. I work with a lot of high-humility leaders who are uncomfortable when I remind them that they're in a position of power. Their response is often "But I'm just Margaret," or "I'm just like they are."

When you have a title of power, you are in power. You have authority that others do not, and most importantly, you have leverage and influence that others do not. It is a detriment to your impact if your nameplate says CEO, CFO, Director, or SVP and you ignore or try to pretend that those letters don't create impact. They do. I hear you; I know you want to hold on to the idea that you are "Just Margaret." But if you're Margaret the CFO, most people are aware that you're the CFO. If you have direct reports, you have power over them, whether you want it or not. Ignoring or minimizing your power does not remove that power. You can be "Just Margaret" in every aspect of your life outside the office, but when you control wages, opportunity, and security, you are more than just Margaret.

This power dynamic plays in our personal lives as well. For example, a parent has power over a child, and a more assertive partner may have power over a less assertive partner.

If you are in a position of power, it's more likely that people will hold back or adjust how they share tough information with you (especially if it is about you).

Self-Awareness

Perhaps you work as a frontline manager. Or maybe you're reading this as a curious team member or human resources professional. Don't go thinking you're off the hook. You're not excused from perception issues just because you're not in a senior-level role. Most of us significantly overestimate our self-awareness, which means we are very likely to think we're not feeding elephants when we are, or that we're more open to receiving feedback than we might be.

Organizational psychologist and expert in self-awareness Dr. Tasha Eurich studied five thousand people over five years, evaluating each participant's perception of self-awareness against their actual self-awareness. She found that around 90 percent of people said they were highly self-aware, but when her team evaluated each participant's behaviors and mindset, the number of people who were genuinely self-aware, from an internal and external perspective, amounted to 10–15 percent of study participants.

Dr. Eurich defines self-awareness through these questions:

- How well do I know myself?

- How well do I understand why I do what I do?

- How do I show up?

- How do I experience things?

It's a strange little mind puzzle, isn't it? It's not likely to be effective to prescribe self-awareness as a solution to the 90 percent of people who believe they're already self-aware. What if, instead of assuming we are highly self-aware, we all simply acted as if we aren't as self-aware as we'd like to be? Let's take the judgment out of it. There's no award for self-awareness, and we're more likely to be lacking than not.

I know that even though I work hard to be trustworthy and approachable, there's still likely feedback my team members won't share with me. Or they wait until later, and I wonder why they waited so long. Even with all the work we've done, I never want to assume that my colleagues are going to be 100 percent comfortable being honest with me. I would rather assume they aren't and work harder to gain their trust.

If you truly want to be someone people feel safe with, assume they don't. Then you can take intentional action to change that.

THE VALUE OF PSYCHOLOGICAL SAFETY

While this chapter is for all of us, I want to continue to talk to those of you who lead people. The way you show up in moments of tough feedback, heated disagreements, and conflicts of values sets the tone for how safe your team members will feel. I want to be very clear: saying you have an open-door policy isn't enough to instill trust from your team. I hear this all the time from leaders. I appreciate the sentiment behind this, but I've often felt that by saying you have an open-door policy, you're also implicitly saying that you could close the door at any time. That's not your intention, right?

High-performing teams and high-value-add teams have consistent characteristics that set them apart from average or lower-performing teams. One of those is a degree of psychological safety. Harvard professor Dr. Amy Edmondson coined the term "psychological safety" in her research on team function as "a shared belief held by members of a team that the team is safe for interpersonal risk-taking."

When working with leaders, here's how I describe psychological safety: psychological safety is the ability to be your authentic self, to fail, to take risks, to disagree, to challenge thoughts, to ask for help—all without fear. In short, it's the antithesis of walking on eggshells.

Note that having psychological safety is not the same as not having conflict. If a client came to me and said they had no conflict or disagreements in their organization, I'd be concerned. That would indicate nobody felt as though they could "rock the boat" and show up authentically, even in moments of discomfort. Psychological safety is the opposite of this scenario.

Building this sense of deep psychological safety starts with us and the risks we are willing to take, and the way we show up when others take risks. To instill a sense of psychological safety for those around us, we need to relentlessly seek self-awareness. We must remember that what each person needs in a situation to feel safe is different. Feedback helps us see our gaps and helps us close that gap. We need to be impeccable in how we show up when things are hard. We need to ask for feedback over and over again. We need to hear it and take action. Karen Eber, Leadership and Storytelling Consultant, writes:

> "When you have psychological safety, all that energy goes to the work. Because you aren't concerned about which version of the leader will show up, you aren't concerned about constructively challenging ideas because they are welcomed. You don't have

to feel like someone will blame you. All the energy is able to flow towards the work. Which leads to better physical, mental and emotional energy. You may be tired from the work, but you aren't drained from extenuating circumstances. We often think there is a big difference between a high performing team and a dysfunctional one. In reality, it is a very fine line. It is dependent on the ability to practice teaming and psychological safety with each other."

As Karen Eber thoughtfully explains, creating that psychological safety is critical—but it's not always easy. That's because we have to start the process by looking *at ourselves*.

Let's talk about the ways we unwittingly erode trust, the blind spots we may have, and what you can do to become someone people trust with difficult conversations.

THE POWER OF TRUST

I hear you, and I trust you when you say you're good, kind, and understanding. As we've seen in several of the stories in the previous chapters, even with those beautiful intentions, we will have people in our sphere who don't feel safe sharing feedback with us. We can influence someone's feelings of trust, but ultimately, we don't get to decide how trustworthy we are. The other person does.

And the reality is, if people don't trust you, they're likely not going to tell you they don't, even when you ask. So how can we build a culture of safety and trust, especially related to hard conversations? One way is through feedback. Gathering feedback isn't just about getting insights for what you can do new or differently. It's an opportunity to invite someone to take a risk, and for you to show them that it's safe to do so. Even if we ask for feedback and someone withholds, how we show up in that moment can lay a foundation for them to share differently next time.

Why is this so important?

Simple: **trust and feedback go together.** Saying you're "open to hearing feedback" and "being committed to internalizing, getting curious about, and doing something about it" are two completely different things.

We all believe we are safe and open creatures. You will earn your team's trust through the way you receive feedback. We'll dive a little more into this in Chapter 10. For now, remember this: **You don't get to decide if you're trustworthy. Other people do.**

SOMETIMES IT *IS*
ALL ABOUT YOU

You've figured out how to recognize that you're feeding an elephant, acknowledge it, and bring it up with the other person or in a group. We've even explored why it's difficult for you to bring up an elephant. But what happens when the challenge is about you? What if something you did or didn't do contributed to the creation of an elephant? What if no one feels like they can tell you?

In conversations about trust, I'll ask, "How many of you would describe yourself as trustworthy?" And of course, everyone raises their hand—except for that one smart aleck who says, "No, I know myself too well. I wouldn't trust me."

As human beings, we overestimate our goodness all the time, and we are all likely to overestimate how easy it will be for others to approach us with feedback or a sensitive issue. In fact, as we discussed in an earlier chapter, our aversion to cognitive dissonance keeps us from registering information that contradicts the way we feel about ourselves.

I've never met anyone who says, "You know what, Sarah? I'm really good at retaliation. When somebody gives me feedback that is hard to hear, I make sure they never think about doing that again." And yet, anyone who has ever received or delivered "360 feedback" has seen this. Inevitably, someone will quickly try to figure out who said what and discredit the feedback, or worse, use it against that person.

Whenever I've had to point out to a leader that their team doesn't communicate because of fear of retaliation, I hear, "Me?! But I would never retaliate!" When they say that, it feels true to them in the moment because their conscious brain would never retaliate, but their amygdala-driven brain sure might.

Most people say—or at least think—that they're nice, so others should be able to bring things up with them. Makes sense, right? To be fair, sometimes that fear of retaliation may have nothing to do with you and may be the result of a previous experience with another leader.

> The bottom line? If you've identified an elephant in your midst, the first step is to look at yourself and see how you have contributed.

SOMETIMES IT'S *NOT* ABOUT YOU

You can do everything right, and it can still be difficult for your team members to come to you with feedback.

If a team member worked for a leader in the past who didn't receive feedback well, it's going to influence how safe they feel coming to you to talk about an elephant. They might need extra time to heal and feel secure in their job and relationships before you can have those conversations.

When I talk about this work with my parents, who are in their mid-seventies, they tell me how wonderful they think it is that organizations are moving toward a culture where feedback can be given and received. "We would never have done that," my mom said. Dad added, "Back then, you respected authority. If something wasn't working, you sucked it up, and you tolerated it."

I don't, however, want this to let you off the hook. There are things you are probably doing (or not doing) that are contributing to your team's feelings of uncertainty or lack of psychological safety. Even if you're sure there are other factors at play, keep doing the work to create an environment where team members can bring vulnerable conversations to you, and that means examining your own unconscious bias.

"You can't be a great leader if you can only lead people like you."

–Gilmara Vila Nova-Mitchell, DEI Leadership Coach

ELEPHANTS AND UNCONSCIOUS BIAS

As designer David Gaider once said, "Privilege is when you think something isn't a problem because it's not a problem for you personally."

We must remember that stakes are higher for some people simply because of who they are, what they look like, who they love, or how they represent themselves. Our society allows some voices to be heard more than others. When we invite feedback and ask people to join in vulnerable, elephant-freeing conversations, we have to make sure the people around us feel invited and safe to participate. We need to focus awareness on unseen areas and bias- clouding perceptions around who participates, how they are participating, and the true inclusivity of our culture.

I was working with a leadership team at a retreat. While discussing team communication, I said, "Something to be aware of is the fact that women are less likely to be heard, compared to their male counterparts." I explained that we are challenged by the double bind of cultural expectation that women need to be nurturing, collaborative, kind, and agreeable. Leadership, as we know, is predominantly defined by stereotypical masculine traits like being strong, decisive, assertive, and perhaps aggressive. Part of the reason why it can be difficult for people to connect with women who show up in the traditional leadership ways is that it breaks the subconscious story they have about what it means to be a woman.

"We all hold these biases. Even I do," I told those at the retreat.

Brian, a senior leader, joined the conversation.

"Sarah, I'm really struggling with this. I hear what you're saying, but I look at this team, and we have three women on it, and I don't look at them as any different. I don't pay attention to gender."

I said, "I appreciate your desire for that to be the reality. I appreciate your optimism of wanting the world to be safe and the same for everyone, but we know it isn't. Let me ask the women. Are you aware that you're the women on this team?"

All the women in the room nodded.

"Brian," I said. "I'm very aware that being a woman changes how people view me. I'm aware of this because of how they treat me and how that is different from my male colleagues."

We also discussed the double bind against men, which can impact their mental and emotional health. Men are expected to be strong, assertive, confident, nonemotional, not weak, and not vulnerable. Those expectations can leave men struggling to understand and manage their emotions. I work with so many male leaders who cannot answer when I ask, "How do you feel?" They simply don't have enough experience or comfort with the language of feelings.

It was a potent moment of realization for Brian. By examining ways that he has been judged based on gender, he was able to conceptualize the influence of bias on his perception.

Look in the Mirror

If you are asking the question "Do I have biases, or don't I?" You are asking the wrong question. Rather, you should be asking, "What am I doing to continually see and understand my biases?"

Unconscious Bias

When you say, "I don't see gender" or "I don't see race," and you believe your words, you have a bias you are not acknowledging. Ignoring diversity is insensitive to the realities of the people around you. Ignoring is not a loftier stance; it's a lack of empathy and understanding. As long as you stay locked into the belief that not seeing race or gender is part of your identity as a good person, you miss out on exploring perspectives that can make you an even better person and leader. If we want people to have vulnerable conversations with us, we have to make sure we don't invalidate their experiences when they share. You have to understand biases so you can work to overcome them and provide support to people who are struggling against prejudices others hold toward them.

WHAT'S NEXT?

Again—trust and feedback are connected. If someone wants to have a conversation about avoidance we've created or fed by something we've done or didn't do, this is essentially a moment of feedback for us. How we receive and what we do with the feedback establishes the environment for psychological safety and builds the trust people need, to feel like they can have these conversations.

Since we've learned how feedback can trigger our stress responses, when someone comes to you to talk about an elephant, pay attention to your physiological responses. And pay attention in earnest, please. The goal is not to be the most unaffected by feedback. Don't try to ignore a racing heart or the feeling that you'd like to shout or run out of the room.

There's much more to asking for and receiving feedback in a way that moves us—and our teams—forward. We'll explore feedback, intention versus impact, apologies, and more in the next chapter.

Get Curious

- In what situations is it easy for me to reflect and practice self-awareness? When is it difficult?

- What can I do more of or do differently to understand potential biases I might hold and not realize?

- What do I do to create safety for others? What do I do (or not do) that decreases safety for others?

10

Receiving the Elephant: Feedback, Intention, and Apologies—Oh My!

A company I worked for held a United Way fundraiser, and instead of getting silent-auction donations from the community, team members donated their own services and talents. There were auction items like Learn How to Knit or Learn How to Make Toffee, or people donated things they'd made.

One of the team members, Alexis, was an accomplished wood-worker and made a beautiful side table to donate. John, the CEO, and Greg, the COO, got into a bidding war over the table. John won.

When John brought everyone together to celebrate how much money we'd raised as a company, he tried to take a good-natured jab at Greg and said, "Wow, you really stuck me with that table, didn't you, Greg?"

John would literally give you the shirt off his back. He will do anything to help his employees succeed. John's intention was to tease Greg. The impact was that he humiliated Alexis in front of the entire company.

When the chief HR officer and I went to talk with John about the conversation he needed to have with Alexis, his reaction was to throw up his hands and say, "That wasn't my intention!"

In that moment, I realized how often I've said that and how often I've heard it, and I could see so clearly how good intentions don't absolve you from negative impact.

HOW TO ASK FOR FEEDBACK

Feedback is vulnerable for everyone involved. Of course, it's often difficult to receive feedback, but remember that it's also difficult to give feedback and be unsure of how the other person will respond. In leading up to asking for feedback, realize the level of trust and psychological safety you've built among the members of your team—or not—will matter. But as a reminder, how you ask, receive, and act upon feedback will increase the level of psychological safety.

- **Ask for feedback a lot**. All the time. Not just once a year during annual reviews.

- **Ask for feedback from everyone**. If you are a leader of people, you need to ask for feedback from the team members you support, your peers, your family members, and your friends.

- **Be specific in your ask**. If you ask for feedback generically, you're going to get generic feedback. Here's an example of asking for feedback on a specific behavior: "I've noticed that I tend to interrupt people in the meetings a lot, and I want to stop doing that and make sure I am listening fully. Would you please tell me if I interrupt you and don't catch it in the moment?" The more specific your request, the more others will pay attention and give you that feedback.

- **Prime your team**. Don't put anyone on the spot when you ask for feedback. Allow for time to think. Say, "Hey, I'm interested in your perspective. Here's what I'm working on. I want you to think about times when you feel like

I've done that well, and opportunities when I could have done things differently. I'd like you to come with one or two examples for our next one-on-one." This gives time for people to process and shows that's you are invested and interested in their thoughtful answers.

HOW TO RECEIVE FEEDBACK

Oh, feedback! Everyone says they want feedback, and they want it directly. I've yet to have someone say, "You know, I'm not a fan of feedback. I shut down, immediately pick it apart, discredit the person who shared, and won't do anything with it when I receive it." More often than not, when faced with feedback—even feedback we want—we might not know or own when we react in ways that aren't always productive. We can easily receive feedback if the message

- comes at the right time,

- comes from the right person, or

- is what we want to hear.

Of course, these perfect conditions rarely, if ever, occur, so we have to set the stage by asking for feedback and prepare ourselves to receive feedback in less-than-ideal conditions.

In his brilliant article in *Harvard Business Review*[2], Peter Bregman lists thirteen ways we commonly respond to feedback, directly quoted below. Which of these have you done? I'm thirteen out of thirteen.

- Play victim: "Yes, that's true, but it's not my fault."

- Take Pride: "Yes, that's true, but it's a good thing."

- Minimize: "It's really not such a big deal."

- Deny: "I don't do that!"

- Avoid: "I don't need this job!"

- Blame: "The problem is the people around me. I hire badly."

- Counter: "There are lots of examples of me acting differently."

- Attack: "I may have done this (awful thing), but you did this (other awful thing)."

- Negate: "You don't really know anything about X."

2   Peter Bregman, "13 Ways We Justify, Rationalize, or Ignore Negative Feedback," *Harvard Business Review*, (February 2019): https://hbr.org/2019/02/13-ways-we-justi-fy-rationalize-or-ignore-negative-feedback.

- Deflect: "That's not the real issue."

- Invalidate: "I've asked others and nobody agrees with the feedback."

- Joke: "I never knew I was such a jerk."

- Exaggerate: "This is terrible, I'm really awful."

Anyone can sit in a room and physically hear feedback, but how we process it matters. Please note that our goal is not to never have these reactions. We're all human. The amygdala has got to work, right? The goal, then, is to catch ourselves in these reactions before we fall into them so we can shift and find a fruitful path forward. When I'm triggered by feedback, I go for walks or take a nap to help calm down my amygdala. I know these tactics work for me—and I find the more I catch myself, the less frequently I have to use them, too. It's like building a muscle. What works for you will be different than what works for me, clearly, but the takeaway is the same.

RULES FOR RECEIVING FEEDBACK

If you want to create an environment of safety, you have to be impeccable with how you seek feedback and how you receive it. And when you aren't—because that will happen, as we all have regrettable events—ensure that you take the steps to repair the relationship.

Acknowledge the feedback

Sometimes, whenever you get feedback, it's valuable to say, "Thank you for sharing your perspective and experience with me." Other times, the situation can be complex enough to warrant an entirely different reaction, depending on the situation or the power dynamics at play. Most of the time when we get feedback, it comes from someone wanting to help us. I want to be clear that if somebody is saying something harmful or outwardly insulting or aggressive, you don't need to say thank you there. Acknowledging and appreciating the feedback doesn't mean you need to take action on it.

Give yourself room

If the feedback you're given is hard to hear and you're not ready to respond, it's okay to say, "This is tough for me to hear because it isn't how I want to show up. Let me chew on this, and I'll follow up with you." Remember, our brain triggers in .07 seconds. In today's society, we're conditioned to try to solve problems right away. But you don't have to! For me, I know that my brain isn't going to be at its best solving problems when I'm triggered, so it's important for me to find that time. If this resonates, try saying: "Thanks for sharing that with me. I need some time to think about it before I figure out what action I need to take."

Follow up

One of the traps leaders often fall into is not following up to show the team member how they've applied the feedback. Whether it's in an email or another one-on-one, take the chance to give your team member an update. You need to work to not get defensive, to not explain, and to not justify. Your follow-up should sound something like this: "Hey, Samaj, I want to follow up with you. Thank you so much for giving me that feedback. I've been think-ing about how you noticed I interrupt women more than men. Here are some things I'm doing to resolve that. I appreciate you telling me, so I can work to improve and would be grateful if you can let me know what changes you've observed or not." Some-times people won't give feedback because they don't think the person will do anything with it. But by following up, you are showing that you will.

Make it visible

The work of self-awareness means that often our insights will be internal and invisible to others. For example, if I am working on not interrupting others, people won't see me catching it in the moment when I do it or afterwards. Also, sometimes you may need to work just as hard with changing the perception of others as you do at changing the actual behavior. Knowing that some behaviors might take time to shift, it's important to identify at least one action you take that would be visible and make a difference to others. Building on the example above, if you catch yourself interrupting someone, instead of just noting it internally and holding back, you might celebrate the catch out loud. For example, "I'm sorry I just interrupted you. This is something I am working on. Please proceed."

Don't go pants-less

Do you need to take action on all feedback? No. I like to think of feedback like a pair of pants. Try them on. If they fit, great. If they don't, then they don't. But don't throw away every pair of pants that's given to you, even when it's thrown at you missing its tags. Sometimes you need to wear an uncomfortable pair to break them in and make them work for you.

There are some areas of feedback that as a leader, you should always explore and find action to take. Anything related to people's sense of psychological and physical safety needs to be taken seriously, as that is one of most important responsibilities—if not *the* most important responsibility—you have as a leader.

The challenge here, as we've discussed, is that we can be quick to dismiss if we don't agree or if we feel threatened. Two questions I would like you to consider in these moments (and really, all moments) are: "What might be true about this that I haven't considered?" and "What might I be doing or not doing that is giving them that perception (regardless of my intent)?"

WHAT IF YOU ASK FOR FEEDBACK AND DON'T GET ANY?

You can't just ask for feedback once, or in the same way, and expect feedback to come rolling in. If your team isn't bringing feedback to you, try one (or both) of these exercises.

The Genie Exercise

Ask your team to imagine they have three wishes to change anything about the team or how you work together. Then ask, "What would those three wishes be?"

The Start, Stop, Continue Exercise

Ask your team, "What am I doing well that you'd like me to amplify? What would you like me to do differently? What's something you'd like me to start doing?"

Whenever I'm working with a team on receiving feedback, I have them do an exercise. First, I have them imagine they need to give sensitive, constructive feedback to someone about something that person has done (or not).

"How do you hope they will respond?" I ask.

The answers are always some variation of, "I would hope that they're appreciative and know I have their best interests in mind," and "I would hope they'd promise to think about it and make some changes."

Then I say, "Imagine that this feedback you are sharing with the person is likely going to be hard for them to hear." And I ask again, "How would you hope they respond?"

Again, the answers include appreciation and action.

Then I ask them to imagine one more factor. "Imagine this person is someone with whom you don't have a desirable relationship."

There's usually a long pause. Then, "I guess I hope they would see and acknowledge that I was sharing this feedback from a place of wanting them to be better."

Finally, I ask, "How often do you show up in this way when people give you feedback?"

The room usually gets quiet for a moment. It's always profound to see everyone considering this. So often, what we expect of other people is different from how we show up; the answer of how we can be someone people feel comfortable with can be found directly in how we want to be treated.

THE LAND OF GOOD INTENTIONS

When it comes to building a safe environment, good intentions aren't enough. It's not that they aren't important, because they do matter. Good intentions are the foundations for action, but not necessarily the actions themselves. And they aren't the only things that matter. We all have times when we're tired, stressed, or defensive, where we'll say or do something regrettable, or other people observe us being negative. But we don't mean to, or we rationalize it, so we like to pretend it doesn't count. As we explored in Chapter 2, we spend a whole lot of time on autopilot. When we get stuck in the land of good intentions, it's difficult for us to see the gap between how we want to show up and the actual impact we're having. **You judge yourself by your intentions, but other people judge you by your actions.**

Intending to be approachable isn't the same as *being* approachable.

Complainers don't see themselves as complainers.

Every morning, I start my day with beautiful intentions of working out and eating well, and yet at the end of the day, I find myself on the couch binging Netflix and eating Double Stuf Oreos. Our intentions don't always translate to actions.

Perception is a Multiplier

If you have a negative relationship with someone, everything you do is going to be through that lens. Conversely, if you already have a good relationship with someone, they're more likely to give you the benefit of the doubt. You can't control other people's perception, but you can work with intentional action to build powerful relationships.

What's the Message You're Actually Sending?

I fell into the habit of telling people how overloaded I was feeling. If someone asked how I was doing, I'd heave a huge sigh and say, "I'm so busy right now!" My intention was to commiserate and be able to share my stress with someone.

Then I noticed I was seeing a lot of pictures of all of my friends at events or on trips together, and I wasn't invited. I felt so sad and left out. Finally, I asked my friend Christine why I wasn't invited anymore. Christine said, "You're always so busy. Whenever we talk with you, it seems like you're really overwhelmed. I don't want to add another thing to your plate."

Whew. While I saw my expression of busyness as something to connect over, I was actually telling everyone that I don't have time for them, and I literally drove my friends away. My impact was completely at odds with my intention.

How We Undermine Our Intentions

Using terms that place others on the defense is a surefire way to undermine your intentions. When you say things like, "Please don't take this the wrong way," "I don't mean to be rude, but..." or "With all due respect," you're essentially telling your conversation partner that what's coming next could be hurtful. Even if what you say next is minor feedback and mostly positive, the defensive mindset you've established can make it harder for the other person to hear your feedback with an open mind.

Another way you may undermined your intentions is to minimize how someone is feeling. Sometimes, it's hard for us to see someone in a state of pain and discomfort, and we'll attempt to dampen the significance of the problem or attach a bright side. If someone comes to you with a problem and you act on your intention to make them feel better by telling them it's not a big deal, your actual impact could be creating shame because you've minimized how someone is feeling and told them they're wrong to feel that way. If you find yourself trying to show someone the silver lining or saying something like, "At least you don't have cancer," or "Sounds like a first first-world problem," stop! Not only can this create additional and unnecessary shame, but it might trigger something else in them. "I don't have cancer, but my dad died of cancer and now I'm thinking about that." Apologize, and listen to how they're feeling and what they have to say.

Working Backward from Impact

All of this might make it sound like lining up your intentions with the impact you hope to have is a complicated act, but often all we have to do is follow the path backward from our intent and keep it simple.

At a mental health conference, I gave a presentation about how we can show up more powerfully for people dealing with mental health challenges. As I invited the audience to engage in this discussion, a woman named Celia stood up in front of the group of three hundred people and shared with us that her son had died by suicide the year prior.

Celia said, "What was interesting was that when I finally felt ready to go back to work and tried to be part of the world again, it was tough because everyone was asking me the same damn question:

'How are you?' I felt like I was in a lose-lose situation. Either I had to step back into the grief I wanted to distract myself from, or I had to lie." She sighed heavily. "I know they intended to make me feel comforted and show they cared, but the impact they were having was that I felt forced to talk about this thing that was so painful."

I asked her, "Did anyone show up in a different way that was helpful?"

Celia said, "Yes. When I came back, one coworker simply said, 'I'm really glad you're here. I missed you.' And that was it. I felt comforted and welcomed by her."

Sometimes it is that simple. Celia's coworker wanted Celia to feel a sense of belonging, so she told Celia she belonged.

STRATEGIES TO MARRY YOUR INTENTION AND IMPACT

We wouldn't head out on safari looking for elephants without the proper equipment. Just as we'd pack up our Jeep with supplies, we can arm ourselves with behavioral tools to make tracking our office elephants easier.

Multiply Your Mirrors

When we're changing lanes while driving, we consult our rearview and sideview mirrors to get a clearer view. When you're working on following through on a desired impact, you can adopt practices to help you see as many of your blind spots as possible.

For example, if you've noticed your defenses go up in a tense situation, ask yourself what behaviors you employed. Were your actions coming from a place of protection instead of a place of partnering? Are you comfortable with that, based on the situation? What might you have done differently?

Another way to get clear about the impact you want to have is to adopt a mirror mantra. The common mirror mantra I hear is "Treat people as you want to be treated." Or even better, "Treat people as they want to be treated." You can use your mirror mantra like a checklist and ask, "Am I treating people as they want to be treated? Or what ways might I not be?"

Here are a few of my favorite mirror mantras:

- "Talk less, ask more."

- "Don't give people a reason to regret meeting me."

- "Be the daisy in the onion patch."

- "Help people see the greatness within that they may not see themselves."

Find a Conscious Copilot

Since we know that it's almost impossible for us to see ourselves clearly all of the time, we need to have someone else looking at the picture with us. Find somebody to be your conscious copilot.

Identify two or three trusted people in your personal and/or professional life who won't be afraid to tell you if you're employing behaviors that go against how they know you want to show up. It might seem like a scary thing to ask, but what I've found is that people are flattered by this request and eager to help. In asking them to be your conscious copilot, you're saying that you trust them and that you trust the way they care about you. The request can be as simple as saying, "I'm trying to work on X. Can you help me see when I'm missing or hitting the mark?" Or say, "When you see me do X, call me out on it."

Jasmine, one of my clients, has adopted "in the moment" words with her co-manager, Aya, that they use to help trigger awareness when one of them isn't showing up the way they want to. For example, Jasmine tends to see complicated issues in an either-or way. When Jasmine does get too linear in her thinking, Aya will say, "Well, you know, let's think about this," and that's the trigger for Jasmine to realize she needs to consider multiple possibilities.

It is important to note that not all riders are created equal. You don't want a conscious copilot who will delight in pointing out when you're making a mistake. You also don't want a conscious copilot who just wants to make you feel good. Your conscious copilots should be people who are curious, compassionate, and most importantly, candid.

WHEN—AND HOW—TO APOLOGIZE

I often joke that we receive more training and instruction when it comes to learning to drive a car than we do in learning how to show up in conversations more intentionally and thoughtfully.

And yet as leaders, if we want to build workplace cultures where people can feel safe, take risks, and bring their whole selves to work, then we need to be equipped and prepared to have more powerful conversations...and be able to apologize simply, effectively, and with sincerity.

Trust and psychological safety at work are built one moment at a time, one conversation at a time, and one apology at a time.

Apologies are one of the most powerful ways people can bond and build trust with one another. They provide a foundation for reassurance that when (and it is *when*, not *if*) regrettable events occur, we'll be able to navigate them together. Regrettable events are when we intentionally or unintentionally don't show up at our best and risk causing harm to the relationship. Even the best relationships experience times that warrant an apology, and they will happen when we least expect them because we're humans.

Knowing how to apologize and take ownership of your impact is a powerful practice, and we've broken down apologizing into its core components.

Name the situation

The very first thing you should do when you apologize is verbalize that you know what you did was harmful. You need to be clear and explicit with the recipient.

Let's visit what this can look like with two sample apologies. The bolded words are the portion where the situation is named.

Not Helpful: "Hey, **I know I snapped at you yesterday**, and I want to apologize. I was having a really awful day and that meeting pushed me over the edge."

Helpful: "Hey, **I want to apologize to you for snapping yesterday**. That's not how I want to show up, but it was how I showed up in that meeting. I want to apologize for the impact that had on you and for shutting you down in that way. You deserve better than that from me."

Both apologies name the situation, but in two very different ways. The "Not Helpful" apology acknowledged the situation in an almost dismissive way, while the "Helpful" apology provided a direct, objective acknowledgment of the situation at hand.

Own the impact

Apologizing and taking ownership of your impact on others is a practice that I consistently see people struggle with in this work.

Many people can get to a point of taking ownership internally, where they can think about and realize they have overstepped and understand their impact was different than they intended. But they might not ever take the step of saying that out loud to the person they may have harmed.

The key parts of an apology are verbalizing and owning your impact. Without those, it's not a real apology. About a month ago, I received an email from a leader in his organization who had attended my workshop on Intention vs. Impact. The email detailed a situation in his workplace where he showed up in a more reactionary way than he would have preferred to. He further shared that following that situation, he spent time wondering if it even made sense for him to apologize.

It was only after hearing about the importance of owning one's impact on others that things clicked into place for him, and he knew an apology to his team was simply the right thing to do.

All,

I sent a separate note to Jess, but I want to apologize for being short with you all in our meeting at 3:30. I wasn't at my best, and I just want to acknowledge that.

What I needed to say was "thank you." You all work very hard, and I know these things aren't easy. We will find the best path forward as a team.

Have a great weekend.

Regards,

Ben

I share this email with you because it is a perfectly beautiful example of what it can look like to take full ownership of your impact and to apologize for how you affected others, *without* explanation of intent.

Revisiting our two sample apologies from above, note that the bolded words are the portion where the impact is named and owned.

Not Helpful: "Hey, I know I snapped at you yesterday and I want to apologize. I was having a really awful day and that meeting pushed me over the edge."

Helpful: "Hey, I want to apologize to you for snapping yesterday. That's not how I want to show up, but it was how I showed up in that meeting. **I want to apologize for the impact that had on you and for shutting you down in that way.**"

Quite obviously, the "Not Helpful" apology has no acknowledgment of harm done. Instead, the apology closes with asking the harmed recipient to provide grace and forgiveness to the apologizer. The "Helpful" apology not only apologizes that your actions had impact on the other person, but it goes a step further to acknowledge the way you may have changed that person's behavior in the moment.

Leave intention out

There are lots of reasons why apologies are hard. Sometimes we might avoid them because saying it out loud means it is real, but the reality is it's been real to the other person the whole time.

Apologies in their purest form should be simple, short, and sincere, but we often want to expand on them to make us feel better, not necessarily to improve the situation we find ourselves in. **Understanding the factors that led to why you caused harm to another is an important practice *for you*, not the recipient.**

We often look at ourselves through the lens of "intention," which can be difficult to overcome. The truth is that when we ask the recipient of a regrettable event to assume good intentions, what we are often truly saying is "their intentions are more important than your experience." Insights from TheBias.com show a culture of centering the aggressor's intent can further marginalize victims and create a culture of blamelessness for those who cause harm. Instead, I like to stay open to multiple possibilities until clarity occurs.

I want to be clear: it's not that intentions don't matter, because they do. If someone said or did something that came from a malicious place, that is a different situation and should be treated differently than if they misspoke. When you become aware of how your impact was different from your intentions, that can direct how you handle your response to an apology. **The bottom line? Good intentions don't absolve you from negative impact.**

Our messages are ultimately interpreted and created by the receiver, and there are times where we will not be able to control or understand the lens through which they receive our apology.

It can be as simple as naively saying something unintentionally harmful to, say, an underrepresented group. When you are called in on your impact from your statement, you have two choices:

1. Center your apology around your lack of knowledge. "I'm sorry that I said _____. You have to understand that I didn't know _____, so that's why I said it."

Or...

2. Respond in earnest and say, "Thank you for calling me in, and thank you for sharing that with me. I'm sorry that my words caused harm. I didn't understand the impact of what I was saying, but I understand it now, and I am committed to doing better."

As humans, we also regularly experience a natural sense of cognitive dissonance that sometimes creates a barrier to recognizing the times where we show up in less than desirable ways.

There will always be moments when we're stressed, triggered, or hurt, and we may act in a malicious or aggressive manner unconsciously (or consciously).

We must be honest with ourselves and honor that we are not at our best when we are experiencing stress. Whether it involves external factors (like, say, a pandemic) or internal factors (health issues or fear/anxiety, etc.), we know we're more likely to be reactive than responsive to others under times of stress.

In these situations, as you examine your intention behind a regrettable event, please understand it's not a question of whether you're a good person or not; it's simply that you're human. And as a human, are you able to notice and own when you aren't showing up at your best? Are you able to see and own when you were wrong? Those are the reflections you need to weave into your regular self-awareness practice.

Commit to showing up differently

People with high levels of self-awareness often come to the idea of needing to apologize on their own. They've identified a situation and realized that wasn't how they wanted to behave, and they are authentic about their remorse. They are clear about how it wasn't in alignment with their values and are able to own it, even if not effectively.

Self-awareness is great and powerful when we can recognize this behavior internally, but those revelations need to come outside of you and be heard by the person who was harmed by your actions.

Sometimes, it's a situation where it's come to our attention that something we did or said unknowingly harmed somebody else. In these moments, get curious about trying to expand your understanding. "Wow, I totally did lash out. Where did that come from?" The learnings from that reflection can help you in future situations to identify triggers or tension points that may drive you to show up as less than your best self.

Often, people will say, "I'm sorry I snapped at you. *I've just been really exhausted lately.*" And then they leave it at that, hoping (or even expecting) that the harmed recipient will be understanding of their situation.

While it's better than nothing, it's not ideal because it centers your excuse, your triggers, and your sense of entitlement to grace. Instead, commit to owning the impact you caused *without* explanation. Do the work yourself to recognize your triggers, and don't verbalize them as an excuse—instead, commit to showing up differently in the future.

We again go to our sample apologies. The bolded words are the portion where commitment is verbalized.

Not Helpful: "Hey, I know I snapped at you yesterday and I want to apologize. I was having a really awful day, and that meeting pushed me over the edge. "

Helpful: "Hey, I want to apologize to you for snapping yesterday. **That's not how I want to show up, but it was how I showed up in the meeting.** I want to apologize for the impact that had on you and for shutting you down in that way."

You'll notice the "Not Helpful" apology is again missing this key component, while the "Helpful" apology acknowledges that while you showed up in a reactionary way in this circumstance, you don't want to show up that way in the future.

Lastly, part of the healing work in relationships is taking owner-ship—ownership of your impact AND ownership of any areas where you may not have been totally clear on your needs. You can ask yourself, "What is something that I maybe haven't shared that is valuable and important to me?" Once you've reflected, if appro-priate, *after the apology takes place*, you can share your insights with the recipient. This can sound like: "Something I haven't told you is that _____ is important to me. This is an important need I have when working on projects like this."

Receive apologies with confidence

I want to challenge all of us: when someone is apologizing to you and you feel safe and ready to receive it, simply say, "Thank you. I really appreciate you sharing that," or some variation. Sometimes we may minimize or dismiss the importance of the situation, either because we are uncomfortable, or because we might not actually think it was a big deal. Instead of acknowledging the apol-ogy, we say, "No worries. It wasn't that big of a deal." If someone is taking the step to apologize, that tells you that it was important enough to them to speak to it.

Ask for a do-over and begin to heal

Sometimes in relationships, I don't think we realize we can ask for a do-over. As my colleague Amy Myers has observed, many of us come from a culture of shame about failures or missteps. Our colleague Gilmara introduced the language of a do-over, and we use this practice internally. And I want you to understand, this isn't a phrase or practice to alleviate us of impact or to try and drive our agenda further. It's not carte blanche to be more assertive or more aggressive. Instead, it's used to clarify and create together.

It's not uncommon that both parties may leave a regrettable situation feeling disheartened. But we can only control how we show up, and there's a lot we can do to show up authentically, with accountability, and in alignment with our values.

And a powerful place to start a do-over is with an apology.

This can sound like "Hey, I would like a do-over on the project conversation we had this morning. I own that I didn't show up as my best, and I apologize for that and for the impact that had on you. After having some time to think about it, I'd like to try that one again. Would you be open to that?"

This approach gives the recipient the choice to be open to a do-over or not, allowing you to both start at the beginning and craft a more powerful partnership through a conversation reset. "I realized after our conversation that I was talking over you. I want to make sure I hear your perspective; can I try that again?"

Note that there is a shelf life for critical feedback, but I don't believe there is a shelf life for apologies. If you're committed to the idea of creating thriving, empathetic workplaces for humans, then creating a regular practice of owning your impact and apologizing with sincerity must be the heart of the work you're doing.

WHAT'S NEXT?

Putting what we've learned about feedback and intention in our back pockets, let's take a moment to crack through one assumption you may have been struggling to put down until now: that you'll get the result you want every time you free an elephant.

Nope.

In some situations, the simple act of noticing you've been feeding the elephant is enough to free it. For example, when we hold an incorrect assumption about a person or a situation, all it takes is gaining awareness of the discrepancy. Other times, taking the step to acknowledge and talk about what you've been avoiding (as a person or as a team) is enough to free the elephant. In situations like these, you hold a good deal of the power to free the elephant.

But sometimes, even if you address and free the elephant—which, again, is the avoidance and not the conflict itself—you will not get an outcome that makes you want to skip happily into the sunset. Sometimes the result of freeing an elephant is setting a boundary. It can mean a change in the terms of, or even ending, a relationship.

Let's talk about this. All elephants are technically free-able because you can overcome your avoidance. But what happens when the outcome doesn't look how we hoped? We'll explore that together in the next chapter.

Get Curious

- What ways have you responded unproductively to feedback?

- Who is someone in your life that could be a copilot to help you close the gap between your intention and impact?

- When was a time when you should have apologized but didn't? How would you do it differently next time?

11

When Freeing the Elephant Goes Differently than We Hoped

The shifting workplace environments where people are becoming more clear about how and where they want to work led one of my friends to reevaluate what it means to lead within his organization. To improve company culture, he wanted to move away from the traditional structure and give his team more potential for autonomy, ownership, and collaboration than they'd had prior. This decision was antithetical to "the way things were always done," and his supervisor was not happy with the new vision. When my friend brought it up to his boss, the idea was squashed without further conversation. It became clear there was a value conflict that was not going to be smoothly resolved.

A few weeks ago, another friend shared that after multiple attempts to strengthen a relationship with a coworker, she couldn't find a willingness on the other person's part to collaborate or connect beyond their technical work. "I really want to improve this relationship," she said, "but I feel like I've done everything I can to hear their perspective, and they continue to dismiss mine. At this point I just need to make it work and be okay that it isn't what I had hoped."

When I heard both these stories, they resonated because they describe common tension points I see, such as people who are passionate about wanting to work differently—including more collaboration, and affording more autonomy to team members— but work for someone with a more traditional style of leadership, which is command and control. Or that a relationship was strained, and one party was unwilling to repair it. Though neither situation avoided the conflict, and rather brought up the questions at hand, the results were still not what they'd hoped.

THIS CONFLICT ISN'T GOING ANYWHERE

If your situation isn't moving forward, you might observe a sustained unwillingness to do the following:

1. **Be Curious**. To free an elephant, we need to take the time to diagnose the real problem instead of settling for superficial answers. Curiosity requires us to consider other possibilities. The solution might not be resolved if somebody critical to the situation is unwilling to be curious.

2. **Make an effort**. Sometimes freeing an elephant can be simple; other times, it can be more complicated, but regardless of the type, freeing an elephant requires a genuine desire to improve the situation, even if that requires improving something about yourself.

3. **Take ownership**. In every situation, everyone involved plays a role in the outcome. We can't move forward if we're unwilling to take ownership or if we're deferring ownership. It's important to note that if we limit ownership to a title and only the leader is responsible for taking ownership of an elephant, we limit the team, and we limit the possibilities.

4. **Collaborate**. Successful relationships are built on mutual trust and respect. A balanced relationship has give-and-take. When someone holds the belief that they alone can fix it, the focus turns to them instead of creating a collaborative solution to free the elephant.

5. **Be willing to change**. Solving problems requires us to take risks, to get messy, to tinker and experiment, and

to step into the unknown. This sometimes means our hypothesis won't be right, but to find out what is right, we might first have to be wrong.

In my experience, when one of these stumbling blocks is present, new elephants can emerge because of the actions and reactions of the people involved. If we don't navigate these moments effectively, people can increase their avoidant behavior because of how a person (or people) on the team reacted, and we create breeding grounds for more elephants to emerge.

It's important to note that at the start of an attempt to free an elephant, it's not uncommon for someone to be unwilling to be curious, make an effort, take ownership, collaborate, or be wrong and then evolve their stance. In one of my first consulting meetings with a CEO, she stated emphatically, "I'm not going to change, so don't try to change me." Eventually, as she saw the potential in making changes to her management style, she was receptive to the work. As we talked about earlier, people don't fear change; they fear loss. The initial fears of loss and resistance are to be expected and aren't the issue. It's the pattern of *sustained* unwillingness that makes it difficult, if not impossible, to properly resolve a situation.

Additional Complications to Consider

A situation can be hard to resolve if the power dynamic is complicated or you don't have allies.

A Conflict of Values

Sometimes just understanding the values involved in a conflict is enough to find another door into the conversation, but sometimes it's a sign that you can't get anywhere. Elephants can't be freed when the values being stepped on don't have common ground.

Seeking to understand someone's values is a hard practice, especially when you're in disagreement, you feel like someone is creating a barrier, or you feel attacked. Remember that seeking to understand is not about validating or invalidating your values. You're not out to prove someone wrong. It's just about coming to an understanding of what makes sense to the other person. It's being nonjudgmental. It's being curious.

A Difficult Decision

Before coming to work with me, my colleague Teresa was a school administrator. She had been recruited to move to a new school from where she was working.

"We had a lot of conversations up front about how I wanted to work, what my strengths are, what I was looking for in a mentor, and the work I'm passionate about," she said. "I felt so great about starting that job, and it was all great until it became painfully clear that I didn't share the same vision or values with the leadership team on a fundamental, ethical level. Once I figured out how far apart we were with our values, I felt like I couldn't speak up anymore because no one saw the problem the way I was seeing it.

This didn't mean I was right, necessarily, but it was clear we were not on the same page."

The few allies she had left the organization to go to other schools, leaving Teresa with a choice: "Basically, I could stay and continue trying to do the best work I could. Or I could leave. I realized that I didn't want to give up what I knew was right. The painful part was coming to terms with the realization that the opportunity wasn't going to be what I had envisioned."

Teresa accepted that she wasn't going to have a lot of allies, but she was going to keep showing up in the ways she thought were important. "I made a choice to work with what I had control of and do my best to act on what I thought was right for the students and the school and consistent with best practices."

STRATEGIES TO NAVIGATE A CHALLENGING SITUATION

There can be great sadness that comes with realizing that the outcome you hoped for isn't going to happen and/or the situation is worse and not better. Much like processing the stages of grief, there are strategies you can use to come to terms with your situation and figure out the best way to move forward.

Seek to understand the resistance—when applicable

Remember that understanding doesn't have to mean agreeing. Establishing that you aren't searching for agreement can lower the heat on this exploration. As we discussed earlier, people don't fear change; they fear loss. Look for the loss, and you're likely to uncover the point of resistance. Common patterns of loss are loss of power, loss of control, and loss of comfort/familiarity.

One of my clients is a financial institution that has been around for several decades. They are on a new mission of innovation, but they have employees who have been a part of the company for twenty-five years and don't understand the need to collaborate with financial technology companies instead of doing what they've always done. The leaders are frustrated with the resistance, but all we have to do is ask, "What might these people be losing?" And the answer is clear. Whether these employees are conscious of their fear or not, it makes sense that they would be afraid that they won't be successful in this new work. Perhaps they worry they aren't innovative or creative enough. Or that they might not have the ability to learn the new software being presented. In understanding the perception of loss, there's a clear path forward for resolution, using training tools and working to increase confidence and psychological safety.

Sometimes imagining the other person's possible losses is enough to give you an effective strategy. Sometimes you can have a conversation and ask, "What are you afraid you're losing right now that maybe I'm not considering?" or "What concerns you most in this situation?"

Accept the reality

It's important to recognize that there may be times when you know a situation will not be dealt with in the way you find most productive. There are some ideals and values that are worth fight-ing for, and other times when you might say to yourself, "Yeah. You know what? I'm not going to die on the sword for this."

There are many different factors that can impact your willing-ness to accept a situation that isn't resolving. You might be more willing to tolerate a situation because you're taking care of a sick parent and don't have time to find a new job, or you're two years from retirement, or you just had a baby, and it doesn't seem worth it to kick up dust. Maybe your skillset has you competing in a narrowed field, or you live in a small town, and there aren't many options. A client had a situation where they didn't leave a job that was laden with elephants until they finished grad school because they didn't have the mental energy to work full time, go to school full time, and look for a job.

There's a difference between acceptance and resignation. Accept-ing reality is not ignoring a situation. It's seeing what's in front of you clearly, weighing the options, and saying, "I'm going to accept that this is what it is and find ways to keep moving forward in ways that don't cost me."

In accepting reality, we recognize that there are always going to be things that are important to us that are not important to other people. That's just the truth. There are conversations you'll be willing to have that may be too difficult for others.

At the end of the day, only you know where you're comfortable compromising or accepting. Sometimes we may feel passionate about an issue, but if we allow ourselves to step back, we might say, "You know what? This isn't worth it. I'm not going to lose sleep over this. I have to work with this person. I know that's just the way they are. They're not going to leave. I'm not going to leave. I'm going to make the best of it." And there are times when we may say, "I need to speak and stand with courage because this is too important. The consequences of staying quiet are far greater than speaking up."

Please make sure that you are not accepting a situation that is truly toxic or damaging to your mental health if you have options for something different. If you have to tolerate a situation like this because the time to change isn't right yet, consider talking with a counselor or mental health professional to process the experience and safeguard your mental health until you can get out.

Choose your own path

If finding a resolution is important enough to you, it's not happening, and you can't see a way to make it happen, you have a choice. Marshall Goldsmith shares three paths in his book *Triggers*. He suggests that you can "Accept, Adjust, or Avoid." Choosing your own path could mean exploring different opportunities within your current situation, but it can also mean leaving.

This is a scary one. Speaking from experience, it sucks to be put into a position where you feel strongly that something needs to be approached differently but you don't have support or power to help the change. It forces you to question what you believe or what you saw for yourself at the organization. It doesn't feel great to feel forced out of a situation, and it's okay that you may have to mourn the fact that reality is different from what you desired.

I've had to help some leaders work through this feeling of loss. They'll say things like, "Our team is capable of so much, and we just can't get over this barrier." It's not just mourning for the impact that they thought they could have. It's also letting go of the promise they saw in the team.

It's tricky because deciding to leave a workplace means stepping into uncertainty, but it is important to realize your self-efficacy. Sometimes people feel their hands are tied because their fear of the unknown is greater than the pain they're in. I've seen many who have underestimated their ability to rise and recover, and it's inspiring when they tap into their truth.

*Questions to Ask Yourself When Deciding
to Address a Stubborn or Potentially
Unsafe Situation*

- Do I feel unsafe?

- Is the risk worth it?

- Is this situation hurting my health?

- Is there a likelihood of retaliation?

- Am I willing to be fired?

Keep the following in mind:

- You can only control what you do and how you react. My colleague Teresa says, "You can't inject understanding or information into people." They're responsible for their learning and their reaction.

- Sometimes a person's reaction isn't about you. Sometimes you just picked the wrong day or something else is going on. This isn't an excuse but can be an explanation.

- There's a difference between being unsafe versus being uncomfortable. People might say they feel unsafe because they're uncomfortable, but being uncomfortable is not the same thing as being unsafe.

I can't tell you what is right for you. I can't tell you what's important enough for you to be willing to make a move. Only you know, and taking the time to get curious about yourself can make things clearer. Clarity leads to conviction, and conviction leads to courage.

YOUR REAL ESTATE IS MORE VALUABLE ELSEWHERE

I was working for an insurance company, overseeing the quality assurance team. I loved managing the people, but managing the process was exhausting and took a lot of effort. I was being trained at Six Sigma and looking at spreadsheets all day. There's an Albert Einstein quote, "Everybody is a genius. But if you judge a fish by its ability to climb a tree, it will live its whole life believing that it is stupid." I was definitely the fish climbing the tree.

The leadership team did have confidence in my skills related to talent and organizational development. My VP at the time told me they were looking to expand and asked me to create a job description for my dream job at the company. Needless to say, I was excited. Finally, this fish could swim!

After lots of conversations, the role was put on hold. Not just on hold, but they had decided to outsource our entire department to another company. At the time, I felt completely dejected. I kept scrambling to figure out what I could do in the company that would be a better fit for my skills, how I could stop feeling like a fish trying to climb a tree.

When I told my mentor, Leah, how I was feeling, she looked me straight in the face and said, "You have to understand that your real estate is worth way more outside of this company."

It never occurred to me that I should or could look elsewhere. I'd been with the company for eight years. I loved my team (we called ourselves Team Awesomeness), and process management tasks aside, I loved who I got to do it with. But I also knew that Leah was right. I wasn't going to find what I needed in the company anymore.

So I started looking. I applied for a leadership development role at ARAG, a legal insurance company. My time at ARAG transformed me as a person and as a leadership development manager and laid the foundation for starting my own company. If Leah hadn't helped me realize that there were more possibilities out there, I would have likely spent a few more years exhausted, burned out, and out of alignment with my strengths and values.

I was caught in the trap of believing there were no other options because I was beaten down by my experience. It's important to realize that when it becomes obvious that it's time to move on, you may be too exhausted to feel like it's possible. If you're seeing a path that could make things easier and the people you work with are unwilling to explore with you, it's easy to become disenchanted and disengaged, but it doesn't mean you'll feel like that forever. My personal rule now is that if I am spending more time and more energy feeling stuck and obligated rather than engaged and energized, it's time take action, even if that means doing what I need to, to protect myself.

As my first executive coach Sharna Fey would tell me, "The pain will push you until the vision pulls you."

TAKE CARE OF YOURSELF

It's important to make sure you're exploring options if you have them. However, if you've considered other possibilities and staying put is your best one, then you'll have to find ways to take care of yourself. If you're in a toxic work environment or a place that is unfulfilling and you don't have other options, that's tough, and can be emotionally and psychologically draining. Here are some things that may help:

- **Seek allies**. It is important to find allies, whether they're inside or outside of work. This is critical because sometimes you just need someone to hold space for you, to validate the way you feel, and to listen.

- **Get your bucket filled elsewhere**. I believe that self-care is whatever you can do in your life to give yourself more positive energy. If work is not fulfilling you, find a hobby, spend time with friends, or volunteer so you can get your bucket filled elsewhere. Create your manual of care, whatever that looks like, to stay connected to your true self.

- **Seek help**. Do you have access to a professional counselor or coach who can help you with what you're going through? Finding outside support can help you decompress and set up strategies for coping or taking action.

- **Set boundaries**. Find ways to limit the time you spend in the situation. Limit your work hours. Leave the office at lunch. Choose who you spend time with when possible.

A final note: I am not suggesting that self-care can remove the harm from working or being in a toxic or abusive situation. It won't. We often talk about how no amount of life hacks or dinners made easier with rotisserie chicken are going to heal burnout or hurt. The hope is that you can find ways that work for you to rest, recover, and protect yourself until the situation evolves and that you can do what is best for you.

WHAT'S NEXT?

I know dealing with stubborn situations is hard. If you're struggling with the fact that an elephant isn't getting dealt with in the way you think would best serve the relationship or the situation, it's because you care. There's something you value on the line. I would rather deal with a situation that's hard because it matters than to wade around in apathy.

In my experience, when we come from a place of compassion and curiosity, there's a lot of room for positive change. Sometimes people surprise you. I have seen many relationships that seemed irreparable turn into healing and productive situations. Other people might not always say what you want them to say or do what you want them to do, but if you can tap into a common ground of intent and figure out how to act on it together, you can free elephants and create something better. At the end of the day, you can control you. Understanding the hand you're playing can give you the clarity to figure out how you need to show up and what you need to do.

Maybe finding clarity and having a brave conversation won't always free the elephant for everyone else, but it can free it for you. And that's worth something.

Get Curious

- What are strategies you use or would add to help in navigating challenging situations?

- What boundaries have you set to protect yourself? What boundaries have you not set that it would be important to start setting?

- How do you want to show up for yourself (and maybe those around you) when faced with situations that aren't getting resolved?

12

Ready, Set, Act!

Now that you understand the concept of elephants, I want to leave you with additional ways to explore these concepts within your company and teams. Theory is great, but tools are better!

I also know that some of you reading this lead teams or whole organizations, you're my fellow human resources professionals, or you work on/lead teams harboring elephants. Hopefully, this book inspires you and leaves you thinking, "Wow. How do we have more of these elephant-freeing conversations? How do we talk about this topic more as a team?"

As the author, I, of course, would like to gently point out that you can buy a copy of this book for everyone on your team (or even everyone you meet). What a great gift! Right here and now, however, I would like to give you some additional tools for freeing elephants by employing micro-actions for macro impact.

Remember that it's not enough just to do a training session or have one conversation. If you want the culture in your organization to be one where behaviors change and curiosity thrives, this needs to be a regular, continual discussion. It's wonderful to begin the conversation and introduce all the concepts we've covered, but imagine what will be possible when you keep talking about elephants and all the interesting ways we show up as human beings.

Many of the following ideas are incredibly simple but can yield revolutionary results, and they've all come from real client success stories or my own experience while leading the organizational development efforts within a company.

APPLY WHAT YOU'VE LEARNED
WITH PLURPOSE

Plurpose? Plurpose, Sarah, really?

I know. I know. You finally got used to talking about an entire herd of made-up elephants, and here I am hitting you with a word like plurpose. But it's one more important term to help you apply everything you've learned about elephants to your team relationships.

> ## *Plurpose noun*
>
> plur·pose / 'plər pəs /
>
> Play with purpose.
>
> Leveraging levity to step into hard work.
>
> *While the team was initially hesitant to talk about the Avoide-phant in the room, when they approached the elephant with plurpose they were able to free her.*

Sometimes, the best way for us to deal with the tough stuff is not to make it worse than it already is. Approaching an elephant with plurpose doesn't mean we aren't taking the elephant seriously or that there's a lack of respect for the gravity of the situation. The power of plurpose is that it provides an entry point that's less shaming and blaming to the people surrounding the elephant. Using language like "I might be seeing an Avoidephant in our midst," or "Sarah, I think I've been feeding the elephant" is a safer way to acknowledge the role you played. No one is going to say, "I've completely avoided this situation because, deep down, I'm fearful of the outcome," but they might say, "Oh no! There's an

Avoidephant sitting on my lap right now, isn't there? Do you see it? This language or approach doesn't apply to every culture or fit every personality. When we are intentional about language, it can keep the heat hot enough to move people but not turn it up enough so much that they get burned. Inevitably, the conversation can lead to deeper insight. "I'm feeding it because I am afraid I'm going to lose my job if I mess this up."

NINE SIMPLE WAYS TO INTRODUCE THE CONCEPT OF ELEPHANTS TO YOUR TEAM

These ideas provide entry points to conversations without judgment. It's not that the heat is totally removed, but when we employ plurpose and explore through the lens of curiosity, we minimize the heat so we can actually have that tricky initial conversation and then continue the conversation.

In their simplest form, none of these ideas are complicated or expensive, but if time and/or budget allows, there are also ideas to add some extra creativity to your elephant projects.

1. Have a conversation about an elephant that is not specific to your organization

You don't have to jump in with a talk about an elephant in your own office. If people don't feel safe yet, pushing them to talk about an issue before they are ready might burn them, and stunt your communication. Your first conversation about elephants doesn't have to be related to diagnosing what's going on with the team.

That might be too big of a leap. Take a little baby jump instead, and talk about elephants that members of your team have run into somewhere else.

The goal of this conversation is to get familiar with the language and think about the concept. Change doesn't come when we put together an action plan.

Change comes the minute we start asking questions.

In fact, as Amanda Trosten Bloom said, "Our culture is created by that which we talk about and do with regularity."

She is right.

The more we talk about something and give it space and time, the more it becomes a part of who we are and how we show up.

Questions to Boost Your Conversation

Think about your personal and professional life:

- What have you observed in others that tells you there might be an elephant in the room?

- What have you noticed in yourself when there's an elephant in the room? What are you thinking? What are you feeling?

- When have you experienced a positive example of how to respond to the elephant in the room? Who was involved? What happened? What was said?

- What can we learn from these situations you've shared? What best practices can we take away from these situations? What can we start applying?

2. Share a monthly email where you explore elephants

This option is a great way to keep the idea of elephants front and center. Set up a monthly email newsletter for your team.

Share common scenarios that might attract an elephant and helpful tactics for setting it free. Explore scenes, like a conflict between two coworkers, a disagreement with a boss, or a project that has gone off track.

Another unique way to approach this is to add an elephant advice column to your existing monthly interoffice newsletter. While working with a past team, we created a column for *Dear GAIL* letters (GAIL = Gremlins, Assumptions, Interpretations, and Limiting beliefs), to discuss the ways a GAIL mindset often creates an elephant. The column had a thumbnail picture of a wise-looking elephant up top, and we wrote fictional letters to illustrate different scenarios. Here's a sample!

Dear GAIL,

One of the challenges I have in dealing with conflict is knowing when to speak up and when to stay quiet. I really don't want to hurt anyone's feelings, so I am more likely to avoid a situation than address it. But sometimes I feel there are times when I should be speaking up.

Sincerely,

To Speak or Not to Speak

*

Dear To Speak or Not to Speak,

You are not alone in your question. Many people struggle knowing when they should "pick the battle," so to speak. Here are three steps you can take when dealing with a possible difficult conversation or conflict:

Confirm. What do you know to be true? What is fact vs. assumptions or interpretations you have made? If possible, ask someone to help you explore these two. It can be very difficult to admit when we may be telling ourselves a story that isn't true.

Clarify. If someone else is involved, what do you need to clarify? Their understanding of the situation? Their intention? Something else?

Cultivate curious conversation. To help you decide if you should proceed or not, consider these questions:

What is the urgency of the situation?

What is the impact to success if I don't say anything? If the impact is insignificant, you might consider holding off, depending on your relationship. However, if it is impacting your ability, their ability, or anyone else's ability to be successful, then you might consider the conversation.

What is your relationship to this individual? This helps guide you in how to approach the conversation should you decide to have one.

Sincerely,

GAIL

3. Bring a physical elephant to meetings

Often when I do retreats for senior executives, I pack a bag of little plushy elephants. At the start of the session, I hold one up.

"Let me introduce my co-facilitator. This is Gail," I say. "There are things we're going to explore that aren't easy for us to talk about, and we might feel inclined to avoid digging into an issue that feels uncomfortable, but if we want to get to the results we're looking for, we need to have these conversations."

I walk around and place a Gail clone on each table as I continue. "Gail is literally the elephant in the room. She's going to sit on your table as a reminder of those avoidant feelings. If at any point you feel like there's an issue being avoided, I want you to pick up Gail as a cue to all of us that it's time to get curious."

Usually, everyone laughs a little, but when I say, "Can we all agree that if somebody picks up the elephant, we'll explore it?" I have full cooperation.

In addition to being a physical reminder of the concept of elephants, since Gail is a super soft, cuddly little elephant, often, the person holding Gail will pet her as they talk. I hadn't expected Gail to act as a tool for self-soothing when I first brought her to seminars, but it's an added benefit that's much appreciated.

Sometimes someone will call out, "Hey, throw the elephant here," and another person will chuck Gail across the room. It's such a simple way to lighten what is already a heavy conversation. But when someone does grab it or ask for her, it immediately signals to the others that this person is going to take a risk and speak to something important. The dynamics and the focus almost always change, and the conversation is often deeper.

Gail allows us to have deep, vulnerable, curious conversations, simply because she serves as a reminder of the things we're avoiding. By having Gail right there on the table, we're all reminded that those avoidant feelings are par for the course. We're expecting them, and we have a Gail in place to help us push past them.

4. Keep a visual anchor in your office

What we talk about with regularity creates our culture, which creates our reality. Something as simple as having visual cues in your office can have a big impact, reminding everyone to be on the lookout for any elephants that might be lurking. In coaching, we call this a "visual anchor." Similar to passing Gail around in meetings, having an elephant figure or item can be a powerful tool.

Consider ordering elephant mugs, desk figures, elephant pens, and other office supplies for the members of your team.

I most certainly employ this tactic in my daily life. I have an elephant necklace I wear any time I do retreats because it grounds me in the work we're doing. It's subtle, and I don't draw attention to it because it's not for the people I'm working with; it's for me. Since so many people know about my relationship to elephants, my studio is filled with elephant prints, sculptures, and carvings friends and coworkers have given me. In turn, I gave my team members silver elephant bracelets they wear as an anchor as we do this work with each other.

5. Create an award

A client recently created an "elephant wrangler" award for team members who have bravely done the tough work of identifying when they have fed an elephant and worked to free it. Even if it's a simple printout or a gift card for a cup of coffee, presenting an award provides the opportunity to say, "I know that wasn't comfortable. I'm really proud of you for taking the time to get clear about your assumptions," or "You spoke with courage and we are grateful for you."

6. Form a group of elephant champions

It only takes 25 percent engagement to gain momentum and shift company culture, according to a study completed by Damon

Centola, an associate professor in the Annenberg School for Communication at the University of Pennsylvania. Enlist a small group of champions who are passionate about this work to strategize ways to continue the elephant conversation and bring this work forward.

The activities of the "elephant champions" are scalable for budget and time. Meetings can be as simple as a discussion over coffee that sets intentions for the month, or as big and creative as some of the tactics I've shared in this list.

At my last job, prior to starting my company, I recruited an elephant crew. We created a fake company with an elephant logo. We planned regular opportunities to bring the concept of elephants to our workplace. In addition to skill-building workshops, we placed elephant footprint cutouts on the floor and posted quotes all over the office. We even produced a video parody of *The Crocodile Hunter*, with a nature specialist tracking elephants in the office, allowing us to name and explain each one in a humorous way.

7. Create an unexpected experience

How can you cultivate curiosity? Create a (safe, minor) disruption, or set up a unique experience in your office without warning. Don't explain it. Observe how people react and where their points of curiosity are.

The elephant crew I worked with arranged for a local balloon sculptor to visit our office. Only our two leaders (who had to give budget approval) were aware of the plan. The artist took up residence in our break room for the afternoon. He created large and intricate balloon sculptures that were well beyond traditional balloon animals, so the work he was doing was impossible to ignore.

As he worked, he kept note of how many people interacted with him and asked questions. People were confused as hell! At first, there were a lot of questioning looks and chatter between employees as they tried to figure out what was going on. Then some people got curious and began talking to the sculptor, asking, "What do you do? Why are you here?" The answer he gave was, "I'm just here to create." Eventually, word spread, and a line assembled outside the break room, with team members waiting to get a balloon sculpture made. Not just for their kids. For them. It was a fantastic lead-in to a discussion about curiosity at the workshop later in the day.

8. Play the (curious) questions-only game

Ideas are often the product of assumptions, so sometimes, when facing a challenge, it helps to brainstorm questions instead of possible solutions. Then you can use those questions to better look at the situation through a new lens. We're all good with what we know (or think we do), but it's hard to have a handle on the things we don't even know we don't understand.

Set a timer for five minutes and say, "Let's see how many questions about this challenge we can come up with before our time is up. No solutions. No answers. Just questions."

Inevitably, what happens is that the first couple of questions that come out are a little leading, and still trying to solve the problem.

But about halfway through the process, you'll start to land on questions that pry open perspectives your team hasn't explored and details yet to be uncovered.

Curious Questions Only

This is a good time for a reminder that not all questions are curious questions. The goal of this exercise is to brainstorm lists of curious questions that are expansive and inclusive, not questions that are limiting and judgmental.

Not Curious

"Why would you do that?"

"Maybe you should try this?"

"Why did you think this was a good idea?"

Curious

"What else could we try?

"What does success look like?"

"What did we learn from this situation?"

9. Or just ask one question

Sometimes, one question can yield a bounty of answers. One of the best ways to clear assumptions when there's elephant activity in a room is to ask this simple question:

"What don't we know about this situation?"

It's an excellent, simple tool to teach your team because they can apply it immediately and use it over and over again.

In the next conversation you have about a conflict or challenge to be explored, ask, "What don't we know about this situation?" That's where curiosity lies.

WHAT'S NEXT?

Now that you have these actionable strategies, my friends, the "What's Next" question becomes easier to answer. It's time for me to set you free into the wild to free your own elephants.

Get Curious

- What would success look like for you to explore this topic at your organization?

- What is something you've seen work to help deepen learning you could apply to your situation?

- What is one thing you want to commit to doing differently to create a culture of curiosity?

Conclusion

Freeing an elephant isn't always comfortable. Sometimes it's scary. Sometimes it's a risk. But in my work with clients and personal relationships, I've seen firsthand how freeing an elephant can have a significant impact on your team, your work, and your life.

A SUCCESSFULLY FREED ELEPHANT

Recently, I worked with Ann, the CEO of a midsize business-to-business marketing firm. Ann was discouraged by her team's poor engagement scores. She felt like her team members weren't honest with her about the challenges they faced and as a result, often under-delivered or missed deadlines.

When I spoke with the members of Ann's team, they confessed their emotional struggles with her management style. Most of her team members were afraid she would retaliate if they said something she didn't want to hear. They often resorted to surface level discussions that skirted around the issues they were facing as a group.

Even though Ann wanted more engagement from her team, she was also avoiding conversations and failing to push further for real answers. If a situation got so bad that she had to bring it to her team's attention, Ann would react in the moment without thinking about her impact, turning what should have been a conversation into a confrontation.

The work environment bordered on toxic, and many of Ann's employees felt hopeless. But I could see the big, bouncing Avoid-ephant wreaking havoc in their office. I knew if we could free it, there were opportunities for healthy change. Most people don't intend to be evasive. We don't usually choose to be malicious, retaliatory, or defensive. Those behaviors often spring up in reaction to triggering situations or come from our shadow intentions. The more honest we can be with ourselves about our triggers, and the more intentionality we can exercise in how we show up, the greater the likelihood we will have the impact that we seek.

Fortunately, Ann was curious, compassionate, and willing to take an honest look at her part in the situation. We started by getting clear about the impact she wanted to have and planned for individual meetings with her team members. At the same time, I worked with her team, asking what they hoped to accomplish in their conversations with Ann.

Sondra, one of Ann's team leaders, was so nervous about her pending conversation with Ann that she became physically sick to her stomach and called out of work. The next day, she mustered the courage to come back, and she met with Ann. Ann and Sondra approached their conversation by fully owning the roles they played in their fractured relationship. They got curious and had a profoundly vulnerable conversation that increased their understanding and compassion for each other. By the end of their meeting, Ann and Sondra were laughing together. Both reached out to me afterward to say, "That went so much better than I thought was possible!"

Ann and Sondra's conversation had a ripple effect on the entire team. It set the tone for the rest of Ann's individual meetings with team members. Ann adopted an open, curious approach to her team's ideas, and her team grew courageous in their conversations with her and with each other. Team engagement scores drastically increased. Processes improved because team members felt like they could point out obstacles and propose solutions. The Avoidephant fled the building, and everyone was happy to see it go. Ann's team became a healthy, productive, cohesive unit. Not only did the work improve, but their quality of life improved as well.

FIVE BENEFITS OF FREEING
THE ELEPHANT

At the end of the day, you want to be a good person. You want to do good work. You want to help other people be better. We all have a fundamental desire for cohesive relationships. Sometimes that means having hard conversations or acknowledging our reactions to triggers and other behaviors that might not be easy to face. It's worth the work. When you access the full power of your vulnerability and compassion, you're showing up powerfully for your relationships with your team, and you're showing up powerfully for yourself.

The results I saw with Ann's team are quite common when people commit to this work. It's possible to turn a troubled team around and foster a healthy and sustainable company culture. Freeing elephants is an investment in being able to navigate conflicts and disagreements more effectively by keeping tensions from growing and building a team's muscle memory around showing up in a healthy way. If you're willing to push past your comfort zone, roll up your sleeves, and get curious, there are great possibilities ahead.

Here are five things you and your team can experience when you free an elephant:

1. **Deeper relationships**. When a relationship faces a sandpaper moment, but we work through that conflict and repair our connection, it's a bonding, powerful process. We tend to interact through transactional moments instead of transformational exploration. When we need to go deeper to communicate something uncomfortable, it's all the more vulnerable, because we aren't used to connecting below the surface. If we allow ourselves to dig deeper into that conversation from an intentional place, we move into transformational exploration. People want to be seen, and they want to be heard. They want to know they add value. My good friend and

motivational speaker Bonny Williams always says, "What comes from the heart touches the heart." Whenever I have tough conversations, I always remember Bonny's words and try to speak from the heart. When you come from that place, you can't help but feel a deeper connection. Welcome to Relationship Building 101.

2. **Better ideas**. Trying to be creative in a room with an elephant means ideas are left unsaid. If team members hold back for fear of being wrong, the team misses out on an opportunity to uncover building blocks for a greater solution. When a team is free to consider all possibilities without having to navigate around elephants, true collaboration is possible. We know that when a group tackles a problem together, not only do they generate better ideas, but they also have a higher level of ownership in the process. People are more likely to contribute to that which they create. If we can truly create an environment where we can talk about anything, even if it's uncomfortable, we're going to produce better results.

3. **Clarity**. Often when we're avoiding something, it's because there are many unknown variables. We don't know how the other people in the situation are going to react, or what the outcome will be. But even when those elephant-freeing conversations don't yield the optimal result, you leave with greater clarity around what's important to you, what's important to the other people involved, what your next steps should be, and what you need to do to be successful. And who doesn't want a little clarity?

4. **Decreased stress**. When we consciously avoid having a conversation about an elephant, it is like an app running in the background, draining our energy. If there's an elephant we're avoiding, we are aware that we are not having a necessary conversation every time we're around the people involved, and every time someone else mentions them. We drag that elephant with us everywhere. Sometimes the elephant sits on us with its crushing weight. We lose the ability to be present with our families, can't sleep, get sick to our stomach, or find ourselves acting from a place of irritability. It's possible to encounter a pretty big elephant, but more often than not, the elephant just feels big. Sometimes when you get to the other side of the conversation, you'll think, "Why was I so stressed about bringing this up?" There's a reason we use the phrase "to get something off your chest." Once we begin to have conversations about the elephant, the elephant gets up and walks away. We can breathe again, start to release that stress, and use our time and energy for more productive pursuits.

5. **Increased self-efficacy**. When working with people to free an elephant, often in follow-up I hear, "I'm glad I did it. I'm really proud of myself for bringing it up." Even if the issue ultimately didn't turn out to be as big as they'd feared, the conversation they were dreading felt huge. And they did it anyway! Suddenly, they have the confidence to advocate for themselves in a new way. That's powerful. When you take a risk to have a brave conversation and survive it, you realize you're capable of so much more than you believed. It's a beautiful thing. Even if you take on a brave conversation and it doesn't yield an

optimal result, you can leave knowing you did your best and showed up intentionally. You've learned something about yourself, and you'll have new tools to apply to your relationships in the future.

IT GETS EASIER...BUT IT WILL NEVER BE EASY

Sometimes people come to me and say, "Of course this is easy for *you*, Sarah."

But the thing is...it's not. When I have an important conversation, I still feel worry. My throat can get dry. My heart races, and I may need to think through it a bit. But that's okay because when we're dealing with relationships, especially those that are important and that come with a true element of vulnerability, they'll never be "easy." But when you establish emotional safety, even the hard talks can become easier. It's a muscle you build over time—one made stronger by stepping into the fire time and time again.

Others continually inspire me by showing up with curiosity and courage—my husband, my family, and my colleagues. For me, I aspire to meet them there and see where we can go together.

GO FORTH AND FREE THE ELEPHANTS!

Great relationships aren't the ones where there's no conflict, but the ones where you can resolve and recover from the conflict and thrive because of it. Where you can step into the fire together and both come out stronger!

Remember that finding this work difficult doesn't mean there's anything flawed about us. It's hard because we're human, and human relationships are complex, but I believe you can do this work. I'm excited about what's available to you on the other side of those elephant-freeing moments. When we approach an elephant with compassion, curiosity, and courage, we're able to dance in the moment with other people in a vulnerable way that opens our relationships to powerful possibilities.

Congratulations to you for taking this time to explore how to show up more powerfully for yourself and those around you. I cannot wait to see what opens up for you when you stop feeding and free your elephants!

Dear Curious Friends,

First, a note of appreciation for exploring this work for your world. I would love to hear what resonated and most importantly, invite your insights to help us evolve. While we are constantly learning, experimenting, and working to expand our understanding, perspectives, and practices, I also know there are limitations based on our own lived experiences, those we work with, and those we learn from. Even in the process of writing this book, new connections and perspectives emerged, especially related to power, systems of oppression, and inclusion. Some of those insights I wove in, and some I am still exploring and will deepen always.

There are big challenges we are facing and need to face as a community if we are to create truly safe and supportive spaces for everyone. A question that continues to drive us and our work is, if we are not able to overcome our avoidance and have conversations about the smaller moments in our lives, how can we expect to address the bigger challenges we face in this world? This book was written to build those steppingstones, to help you deepen your self-awareness, clarify what is important to you, seek to understand what is important to others, and to start and receive courageous conversations.

I am deeply grateful for you and look forward to continuing the conversation.

With love,

Sarah

PS: you can connect with me on social media @sarahnollwilson or send me a direct email at Sarah@sarahnollwilson.com.

Looking to deepen your journey in understanding how to navigate the feeding of elephants in your world? **Check out www. sarahnollwilson.com/elephants.**

You will find a companion workbook, online training, and additional information on how we can partner with your organization.

Acknowledgments

When setting out on this journey, I never assumed it would be easy, but I can honestly admit that at points, I underestimated the physical, mental, and emotional highs (and lows and all the places in between). Do not let my name on the front cover fool you into thinking I accomplished this alone. I was never alone, and through the entire journey, I had an incredible group of humans supporting me, supporting the work, and helping bring this book to life (along with a healthy amount of Double Stuf Oreos). To sit here and try to find words to describe my gratitude and appreciation feels nearly impossible, but here we go.

I lovingly describe my mind as a brilliant constellation of ideas that explode and connect faster than my fingers can keep up. The pieces were there, but the path was unclear. My brilliant, patient, and thoughtful Scribes, Allison Larkin and Jessica Burdg, guided me and helped me uncover the path and the places to put the pieces. A dream team in the truest sense.

Translating ideas into a book is very different than designing learnings and presentations. Allison, when looking at a literally blank slate and a head full of ideas, you held my hand, cocreated the foundation, and helped me breathe life into the elephants. You were the calm in the chaos. And there was a lot of chaos at times. You pushed me, cheered me, and helped me own my voice. I cannot imagine starting this journey with anyone else and will forever be grateful that you chose me.

Stepping into a writing process that was nearing the finish line without knowing the author or the topic is an act of courage. Jessica, in a time when the entire world felt uncertain and clarity was fading, you stepped in and not only guided me to the finish but helped me go further than I could have imagined. Our conversations went deep, and the work followed. You helped me simplify the complex, lean in more courageously, and most importantly, stood in the heat with me. Walking across the finish line with you is an absolute gift.

Maggie Rains, Donnie McLohon, and Neddie Ann Underwood, my relentlessly helpful publishing directors, you helped keep the train on the track while ensuring the engine wasn't burning out. You were always encouraging and compassionately nudging. Writing a book while building a company during a pandemic might not have been the best choice, but you cheered me on until the end.

This book wouldn't exist without Dr. Cris Wildermuth. Cris, not only did you introduce me to the work of Adaptive Leadership so many years ago, but you also taught me how to spend more time on the balcony, to hold steady in the heat, and to know when I needed a lead goose. Little did you know back in that class together that you gave me the seeds that would bloom into these practices. I will never forget the belief you had in me when I couldn't see it myself.

We have traveled the world together, created together, had panic attacks together, and cried and laughed together more times than I can count. You are family to me, and I cherish all of the domains we purchase after our many late-night brainstorms. Never forget that you are freakin' brilliant.

They told me people only get one chance for a first time read, so use those wisely. Teresa Peterson, Amy Myers, Stephanie Chin, Gilmara Vila Nova-Mitchell, and Vicki Flaherty were gracious enough to read the manuscript throughout the process to help shape the ideas and the words as well as future work.

Teresa, little did we know when our paths crossed so many years ago that we would end up cocreating this unique island together. Your thumbprints are everywhere in this work, and I am grateful to have you as a copilot as we orbit learning together. You help deepen everything we do.

Amy, your attention for detail and clarity of concept complements my creative brain in ways that feel almost magical. You advocate for what is right, push us to work smarter, and are not afraid to remind me of my boundaries, especially when I need them most. Thank you for saying yes and helping us smooth out those waves.

Stephanie, our conversations always embody everything this work stands for—compassion, curiosity, and a whole lot of candor. We sit in the heat together on topics that are important but not always easy. You help me to see edges of my limitations, gaps between what I intend and the actual impact, and where my sprinkles can be powerful. I'm forever grateful that we can be our beautiful messy selves together.

Gilmara, Gilmara, Gilmara...you are a gift that keeps on giving. From our first conversation, you showed up authentically and beautifully human. My world and this work are better because of you. The lessons I have learned from you and continue to learn have expanded my view in a multitude of ways. In many ways, I feel like we are just getting started, and I cannot wait to see what the future holds.

Vicki, you can see and speak truth, poetry, and love in all around you. There is something magical about the way you view the world and the words you use to describe it. Delicious, as you might say. You took me under your wing, and now we get to fly side by side together. I always feel truly seen when I am with you and strive to hold space for others in the same way. Magnificent beyond compare.

Team SNoWCo and partners, past, present, and future, I always dreamed of creating a company that was built for the humans it served but wasn't sure how to do it. Brick by brick, we laid a foundation together, dreamed about what could be possible, and began to make it a reality. We have each other's backs and push each other to greatness without sacrificing ourselves in the process. Amy, Teresa, and Gilmara—see above 😊. Kristin, the anchor to my buoy, even across the ocean, we have each other's backs and will always fight fiercely for each other. Kaitlyn, your speed and smarts are making the future I once dreamed of a reality. Pushing us to see beyond and within, the next chapter is brighter because of you. Zach, you were the first. You took a chance, and you made this company a team. We've both come a long way, and I cannot wait to see where our journeys take us. Rachel, from our first conversation at Panera to a sisterhood, you helped me understand that I could be and was a writer. A gift I will never be able to thank you enough for giving me. Aleesa, from our adventures in Morocco to the storage room, watching you step into your power has been such an honor. Memorea, I love you, madly, deeply, and truly. A ray of sunshine even when the world feels cloudy. We started in the classroom, and now we get to change the world in the boardroom. Katie, often an ear for when I felt lost, reminding us that everything is content and being the voice of confidence in the beginning when I needed to hear it the most. Mary, you are the bold charge of energy and wisdom that has pushed me to understand, think about, and love running a business. You are the friend, confidante, and mentor every founder needs. Nathan, you bring the magic to the page and make the abstract concrete. Another mirror to reflect back and help people on their journey. Sharon, your ideas are expansive and your support heartfelt. I am grateful for our paths crossing and now weaving together. To Kat, Bridget, and the team of Project7 Design, you made this company feel real even before it started and create designs not only for who we are but who we are becoming. I'm grateful to have fellow boss ladies to cheer on and be cheered on by. Ms. Rachel Sheerin, whew, what to say. We remind each other how important it is to stay true, to stay real, and to be yourself. I'm so glad I get to crush it with you. And finally, Nick, not only my husband, my support, but the magic behind the camera...I'm at a loss for words for how important you are to me. I'll try again at the end of this section.

Living during a pandemic was challenging in ways many of us have never experienced. For me, trying to create and write required support, physically, mentally, and emotionally. To that end, love to my ridiculously smart, thoughtful, and enviously well-dressed therapist, Dr. Danah Barazanji. You help me to see things about myself I did not know existed, to let go of things that are not serving me, and to love my big, beautiful, busy brain. I believe everyone should go to therapy, and I hope they all have someone like you.

Halfway through this process, I developed the lovely condition of a frozen shoulder—which, for those unfamiliar, means I moved from six months of severe pain, to six months of severe pain and extremely limited range of motion, to a seemingly endless journey to regain everything. You can imagine that at best, it made writing this book slow, and at worst, physically and energetically painful. I don't think anyone plans to include their physical therapists in a book acknowledgment, but I would be remiss without giving a huge thanks to Abby Gillard and Judd Landers for helping get my arm from –4 degrees mobility to full range. There were a lot of tears and an equal amount of cussing along the way, but I'm grateful that I could get back to writing, even with limitations.

To my colleagues past and present, who joined my curiosity in how we can show up differently for ourselves and others: I am eternally grateful for the conversations, the emails with stories or resources, the text check-ins, and the long walks and talks. I have been fortunate to be shaped by so many people and firmly believe that in every single interaction we have, we create impact. So if you are reading this and if we have connected, please know that you have impacted me. A special shout-out to the original elephant crew at ARAG and the last bosses I ever hope to work for, Lisa Wolf and Erin Barfels. You both believed in me and gave me the space to discover new possibilities, even when my methods seemed strange. And you taught me that love and leadership actually do go hand in hand.

An idea is just an idea until you have others try it on, explore it, and expand it. Then it becomes a reality. To my courageous, compassionate, and curious clients who choose to show up powerfully for themselves and those they serve, I hope my impact on you can match the impact you have made on me. Walking along in your journey of discovery is a sacred role, and to be invited on so many journeys has been one of the greatest delights of my life.

Something I try not to take for granted but know that I often do is my family and my family-plus. Mom and Dad...well, it looks like I finally did something with that theatre degree! From early on, you taught us that we should never judge someone until we walked a mile in their shoes. You taught us to care for everyone who crossed our paths and especially those that others ignored. You taught us that everyone deserved to be loved, cared for, and respected. I understand now in all your lessons that you were teaching me to be compassionately curious, because to be curious about someone is an act of care and love. Your support for my dreams has never wavered. You have always been eager to hear how each presentation goes and want to read and hear all the feedback. Having you ask repeatedly, "What feedback have you heard about your event, Sarah?" is such a sweet gift. I know how proud I make you because you tell me all the time. I am deeply fortunate to have you always and forever on my side. We laugh hard and love harder. I love you both so, so much. - Sam

Okay, sibling crew: Becky, Rachel, Drew, and Dominic, thank you for all the years you "let" me follow you around the house talking your ears off. Little did we all know it was just giving me practice. What we have as a sibling group is special. Really special. We celebrate when one of us wins, and we cry when one of us loses. We have stories that go way back, and we have stories that are yet to be written. Different in our own ways, we are forever connected as empaths. Feeling our way through the world, we always find each other. To my siblings-plus, Dan, Randy, Allison, and Mariana, our family became better every time one of you joined. You all bring a different flavor to this recipe we call the Noll Family. While we are family by law, the truth is, we are family by heart. I love us and what we have.

To the Wilsons—Marietta, Rick, Jess, Jeff, and girls, I was excited to finally become an "outlaw" with your family. You've always welcomed me and accepted me as one of your own. You've supported my journey and been patient with my extroverted energy. There are so many horror stories out there of what it's like to have in-laws, and our relationships bust each of those myths, and I am forever grateful to have you as family. I love our extravaganzas and the joy we get out of just being together.

One of the greatest and most important roles I have the honor of being is Aunt Sarah to this amazing crew of niblings—Olivia, Ryan, Monica, Sebastian, Ben, Delaney, Santiago, Evelyn, Sophie, and Elliott. You bring so much life, creativity, and joy to our lives. From navigating your first steps, to playing hide-and-go-seek or games together, watching you grow and find your way as adults is overwhelmingly amazing. Our lives are fuller because of each of you. My hope is you each find your way, you own your gifts, and you never stop wanting hugs and to hang out. I adore and love you all more than you will ever know.

My darling Nick. I saved you for the end because quite frankly, the tears become overwhelming when I sit too long in my love and appreciation for you. You are the Donk to my Peach, the Jack to my Sally, the Fry to my Leela. When I was thinking about starting my own company and asked you if we were ready for such a risk, you looked me in the eye and replied calmly, "I've just been waiting for you." When I came home from work that last day, you met me on the stairs with flowers and a prepared speech about how proud you were of me. When I said I think it's time to write this book, you said, "Whatever you need." You are simply incredible. You quiet my saboteurs when they get too loud, you celebrate the victories big and small, you make me laugh harder than anyone, and you never get in the way when I think we need donuts for dinner. With you by my side, I fear nothing but losing you.

About the Author

Sarah Noll Wilson is on a mission to help leaders close the gap between what they intend to do and the actual impact they make. Through her work as an executive coach, an in-demand keynote speaker, a researcher, and now an author, Sarah creates a safe, honest environment, preparing people to deal with real-world conflict, have more meaningful conversations, and create purposeful relationships. Sarah believes there is too much unnecessary suffering and stress when it comes to relationships, especially in the workplace, and what is most rewarding from her work is empowering leaders to understand and honor the beautiful complexity of the humans they serve.

With fifteen-plus years in leadership development, Sarah earned a master's degree from Drake University in leadership development and a BA from the University of Northern Iowa in theatre performance and theatre education. (No wonder clients love the energy she brings to their teams!) She is certified in Co-Active Coaching and Conversational Intelligence, and is a frequent guest lecturer at universities. When she isn't helping people build and rebuild relationships, she enjoys playing games with her husband Nick and cuddling with their two fur babies, Seymour and Sally.

To learn more about Sarah, her colleagues, and their work dedicated to building workplaces for humans, visit www.sarahnollwilson.com.